Marx in Management and Organisation Studies

This book introduces new approaches that deploy concepts from Marx's critique of political economy to renew the study of labour, value and social antagonisms in the broad area of management and organisation studies.

Exploring established and emergent strands of Marxian theorising inside and outside management and organisation studies, it delves into, beyond and behind the 'hidden abode' of production to examine a range of issues including the relationship between the workplace and the market; the relationship between conflicts at work and wider social and political movements; the role of class, gender and race in capitalist society; and the interconnection of work and labour with the environmental crisis.

The book will be of interest for academics, postgraduate students and researchers interested in radical perspectives on work, organisation and economic life. Representing both a critical introduction to existing theories and a theoretical contribution to the development of the field of study in its own right, it condenses challenging ideas into a short, readable volume without losing their complexity or sophistication.

Frederick Harry Pitts is Senior Lecturer in Work, Employment, Organisation and Public Policy at University of Bristol, UK.

Routledge Focus on Business and Management

The fields of business and management have grown exponentially as areas of research and education. This growth presents challenges for readers trying to keep up with the latest important insights. *Routledge Focus on Business and Management* presents small books on big topics and how they intersect with the world of business research.

Individually, each title in the series provides coverage of a key academic topic, whilst collectively, the series forms a comprehensive collection across the business disciplines.

Organizations and Complex Adaptive Systems
Masha Fidanboy

Managing Complexity in Healthcare
Lesley Kuhn and Kieran Le Plastrier

Work Organizational Reforms and Employment Relations in the Automotive Industry
American Employment Relations in Transition
Kenichi Shinohara

Qualitative Management Research in Context
Data Collection, Interpretation and Narrative
Bruno Américo, Stewart Clegg, César Tureta (eds.)

Marx in Management and Organisation Studies
Rethinking Value, Labour and Class Struggles
Frederick Harry Pitts

For more information about this series, please visit: www.routledge.com/ Routledge-Focus-on-Business-and-Management/book-series/FBM

'Value has long remained absent or at best marginal in critically oriented organisation studies. In this timely book, Frederick Harry Pitts argues that we cannot avoid addressing this notion to confront the current multiple crises of capitalism. He then guides us into recovering Marx's critique of political economy to grasp how objects, people and relations acquire worth (or not) under capitalism. This exciting journey into valorisation, class composition, metabolic rift and social reproduction sets up a renewed intellectual and political agenda that no organisational scholar committed to struggles for change should miss'.

Patrizia Zanoni, *Professor and Chair in Organisation Studies, Utrecht School of Governance, the Netherlands*

Marx in Management and Organisation Studies

Rethinking Value, Labour and Class Struggles

Frederick Harry Pitts

Routledge
Taylor & Francis Group

LONDON AND NEW YORK

First published 2023
by Routledge
4 Park Square, Milton Park, Abingdon, Oxon OX14 4RN

and by Routledge
605 Third Avenue, New York, NY 10158

*Routledge is an imprint of the Taylor & Francis Group,
an informa business*

British Library Cataloguing-in-Publication Data
A catalogue record for this book is available from the British Library

Library of Congress Cataloging-in-Publication Data
Names: Pitts, Frederick Harry, author.
Title: Marx in management and organisation studies : rethinking value,
    labour and class struggles / Frederick Harry Pitts.
Description: Abingdon, Oxon ; New York, NY : Routledge, 2023. | Series:
    Routledge focus on business and management | Includes bibliographical
    references and index.
Identifiers: LCCN 2022017302 (print) | LCCN 2022017303 (ebook) |
    ISBN 9781032057248 (hardback) | ISBN 9781032057262 (paperback) |
    ISBN 9781003198895 (ebook)
Subjects: LCSH: Marxian economics. | Value. | Labor. | Organization. |
    Management.
Classification: LCC HB97.5 .P5128 2023 (print) | LCC HB97.5 (ebook) |
    DDC 335.4—dc23/eng/20220602
LC record available at https://lccn.loc.gov/2022017302
LC ebook record available at https://lccn.loc.gov/2022017303

ISBN: 978-1-032-05724-8 (hbk)
ISBN: 978-1-032-05726-2 (pbk)
ISBN: 978-1-003-19889-5 (ebk)

DOI: 10.4324/9781003198895

Typeset in Times New Roman
by Apex CoVantage, LLC

Contents

1 Introduction

From critical management studies to the critique of political economy

Introduction

Crises throw into stark relief the underpinning material and economic dynamics driving capitalist society—including, today, that of *value* as the category through which worth is placed on people, things and activities. The question posed in this book is to what extent Marx's critique of political economy (CoPE), and in particular Marxian value theory, can help management and organisation studies comprehend and critique these dynamics. Much of the work on the chapters that follow was completed prior to the upheaval caused by the COVID-19 pandemic. Subsequently, in the context of the COVID-19 crisis—itself in effect a continuation of the long period of market and political turmoil that began in 2008—there was an increasing interest in the topic of value and the different objective and subjective processes that articulate its relationship with production and organisations within and beyond the workplace.

This extends to the commanding heights of Western capitalism. At the tail end of 2020, the former governor of the Bank of England, Mark Carney, delivered the British Broadcasting Corporation's prestigious Reith Lectures.[1] As the world endured the continuing consequences of the COVID-19 pandemic, Carney chose a topic that to a general audience might have seemed somewhat obscure: theories of value. The lectures, subsequently published as a popular book, criticised mainstream neoclassical theories of value based on the subjective appraisal of the utility of different goods, services, government priorities and forms of expenditure.[2] These subjective approaches, Carney argued, see value as relative, not absolute, resting in the eye of the beholder and expressed via the medium of market price.

He suggested that such a concept of value had driven poor public policy, causing or exacerbating the key crises of our time. Undervaluation of care work and underinvestment in health services constrained the response to the COVID-19 pandemic. The valuation of increased economic growth

DOI: 10.4324/9781003198895-1

above all other considerations has put capitalism on a collision course with ecological limits sparking the climate crisis. The speculation and overin-flated valuation of financialised forms of investment and revenue-raising, meanwhile, generated the conditions for the 2008 financial crisis and its subsequent aftershocks. Carney's suggested solution to these failures of valuation and the crises they cause is to cast aside the abstract, subjective theories of value associated with neoclassical economics and return to the more concrete objective theories of value espoused in the classical political economy of Adam Smith and David Ricardo, and within at least some read-ings of Marx. Here, value is seen as inherent to forms of economic activity and the things they create, rather than relative to the worth assigned them by individuals and institutions in market transactions.

These theories focused on policing what Mariana Mazzucato calls the 'production boundary': a rhetorical and analytical tool for distinguish-ing individuals, groups and forms of economic activity that are either productive or unproductive of value.[3] Such approaches have historically seen value as a substance produced and possessed by certain classes and groups. Where at the point of capitalism's ascendancy early mercantilists debated whether value was produced and realised within national bor-ders or between those borders as a result of trade, later, twentieth-century debates raged between socialists who saw value produced by workers in their workplaces and neoclassicals who saw value generated in markets through consumption.[4]

Proposing a return to this theoretical inheritance, it was certainly brac-ing to hear such a senior player in the world of finance make such strong criticisms of what has passed for economic common sense in the contem-porary age. Carney is certainly correct to critique a narrowly neoclassical approach to public policy based on utility maximisation through markets, and a renewed focus on labour and how wealth is produced would certainly be a welcome consequence of a return to more 'objective' theories of value. But Carney's call for a return to objective theories of value only tells half the story of how the world has unravelled in the years since the Great Reces-sion, and misses the antagonistic politics of value that have characterised the present age of populism. In particular, it does not fully capture the extent to which the post-2008 crisis period has been characterised precisely by a poli-tics of value based on the search for a more concrete notion of worth rooted in particular people, places and forms of productive activity.[5] The celebra-tion of certain groups as more productive than others has been a recurring feature of populism on both left and right.[6] Posing the hardworking national 'people' against a succession of purportedly 'unproductive' outsiders, the post-crisis period saw right and left of the political spectrum alike police the 'production boundary' anew.

Whilst subjective theories of value undoubtedly contributed towards the 2008 crash by distorting incentives for markets and states alike, the reaction to the crisis has seen things swing the other way. As the neoliberal age has waned, and with it the dominance of subjective theories of value, the political mobilisation of objective theories of value over the long post-crisis period has tended to locate the problem with capitalism in the abstract, global movement of money and markets. This politics locates value as a 'substance' concretised and contained within national borders. Offering a persuasive alternative for activists and electorates suspicious of the seemingly abstract economy of global capitalism, objective theories of value that concretely root the worth of things in specific people, places and things have underpinned the populist insurgencies of the better part of a decade. Such an understanding of production and trade as a zero-sum game has guided Brexit on the right and ideas around 'Lexit' on the left, as well as Trump's revanchist project of repatriating manufacturing and closing the trade gap with China in order to 'make America great again'. The populism associated with these attempts to police the 'production boundary' has driven a divisive, post-truth politics that has fragmented the international order and placed liberal democracy in peril. At the heart of this political crisis lay a series of claims informed not, as Carney claims, by the abstract and subjective theories of value that have constituted economic common sense for decades now, but rather a sentimental attachment to objective 'substance' theories of value as something rooted in concrete people, places and things.

Across right and left of the political spectrum, these different politics of value diverge in terms of motivations and results but share in common some core formal similarities in terms of the way value is understood, its connection with work and production theorised, and the kind of policy proposals this generates. Notably, all focus their critiques on the apparent abstraction externally imposed upon an otherwise pure productive capitalism by outside financial and economic dynamics located at the global level beyond the local or the national. Value, here, is taken to be an objective category created in certain forms of productive activity rooted in time and space. The problem with the economy is taken to be the specific way in which the value that results from production is valorised, circulated and appropriated beyond the workplace in the market at large, between different individuals, groups and institutions. Hence, in common with Carney, the aim of these approaches is to rescue what is concrete, objective and productive from the abstract, the subjective and the unproductive, albeit by means of a critique of the movement of people and things in the sphere of circulation. Contrary to Carney's call for a more objective approach to value to define political and economic debates in the present day, these notions of value have in fact been those that have most strongly shaped our own time, narrating the shift from an open, globalised, neoliberal political economy to a closed, national-protectionist, postliberal one.

However, rather than rescuing the concrete, as Carney intends, the practical consequence of this politics of value has been to leave the world of work untouched as the point where value is produced, seeing the problem with capitalism, and the site of public policy, as resting in the distribution and circulation of value instead. Thus, the identification of a problem, and the consequences that follow, results in the proposal of certain policy solutions. In this way, different understandings of value can be seen to have different political and practical implications—just not quite in the way that Carney imagines. The theories presented in this book, meanwhile, enable us to think through how value, as both a social and economic category, is conceived of politically; the implications for the politics of work and its futures; and the consequences of different perspectives on value for the production of policy around work, employment and economic life more broadly. Together, these approaches show that, rather than what in Carney's terms would be a purely 'subjective' theory of value focused on processes of market exchange, or a purely 'objective' theory of value focused on processes of material production, it is necessary to tread a 'third way'. This third way is indebted not to marginalism or neoclassicalism, nor to the classical political economy of Smith and Ricardo, but to Marx's CoPE—if not, necessarily, 'Marxism' more broadly.

From the perspective of this book, Marx's innovation was not a purely objective 'labour theory of value' like that of the classical political economists, but a *monetary* theory of value for which the historically decisive aspect of capitalism is the organisation of production towards the valorisation of value through the exchange of commodities by means of money in the market. This reconnects value and labour, reading each through the prism of the other. From this perspective, therefore, it is important to understand the labour process from the vantage point of the valorisation process as a whole. The theories covered in the chapters that follow reveal that value organises labour insofar as the latter is geared towards the production of the former in capitalist society. At the same time, they also read value through the prism of labour, insofar as the latter is a form in which the former appears at a specific stage of the process of its valorisation.

Together, they imply that we cannot clearly separate the labour process through which the things that carry value are produced, and the overall valorisation process through which the invested capital is expanded and the surplus appropriated as profit. The latter is not external to the former, as various socialist experiments assumed, retaining the capitalist labour process under a different set of value relationships with the state in control. The valorisation process is not imposed upon production, distorting the world of work, as contemporary critiques of financialisation and rentierisation might contend. Rather, the two represent moments of a social and economic whole that are internally, rather than externally, related. Such an understanding embraces both 'subjective' elements—insofar as value is ultimately expressed in the monetary exchange of the products of labour, but also insofar as there is a constant struggle over its terms—as well as 'objective'—insofar as the pursuit of the successful exchange of the product of labour in the market organises the process of production in conformity with prevailing expectations driven by price dynamics set in the sphere of circulation. In this way, the subjective elements of value captured in neoclassical accounts pass over into the kinds of objective characteristics captured in classical political economy. The distinction of Marx's CoPE is that it represents a third way between the two, presenting an internal critique of the latter that prefigures the innovations of the former.

Marx's value theory thus presents an understanding of the dialectical relationship between the subjective—represented in the desires of humans for certain needs and wants accessed through exchange, as well as the struggles of workers for recognition through and by means of claims on the value of their labour—and the objective—in other words, how these subjective desires and struggles for recognition pass over into more durable forms and purposes that stand apart from human agency and control and come to structure how we produce, consume and organise work and economic life. This is not a mechanical or deterministic framework but an open and contingent one within which workers have a power to resist and reshape the terms on which their labour and its results are measured, managed and valued and within which companies have the capacity, within certain market conditions, to measure, manage and value labour through more-or-less responsive and consensual means. Our common humanity distinguished and set apart from the animal kingdom by our work upon the world, for better or for worse value represents the modern-day means through which the social recognition of that productive activity is mediated. Within the measures and monetary forms in which this is expressed, workers and other actors find space to struggle and bargain for better across lines of identity and difference. Towards this practical end, this book introduces theoretical means of removing the veil on value as a purely economic form of objectivity, helping reveal it as a social, political and institutional category combining the objective and subjective elements of which Carney speaks. We will conclude that creating opportunities for countervailing power to contest the terms on which our work and the world are valued, rather than seeking to normatively fix them in advance by means of either markets or the state, is the means to address the manifold crises that Carney highlights.

Critical management studies and the CoPE

Charting the aforementioned 'third way' through the impasse of value that Carney identifies, this short book maps some of the different ways Marx's CoPE has been taken up and adapted by scholars researching work, employment and economic life in capitalist society within the context of what we can call, for convenience's sake, 'management and organisation studies' (MOS). Responding to calls among critical MOS scholars for a greater engagement with value as a category of critique, the book charts some of the possible new directions this reception could take in response to key global and societal challenges and conflicts around class, gender, race and ecology. It does not exhaustively document every empirical or theoretical aspect of the selective cross section of perspectives surveyed, with a focus specifically on how they approach the relationship between value and labour and their interconnection with class struggles and social antagonisms. The choice of examples used to illustrate their actual and potential uptake in MOS is similarly selective and subjective. The book does not necessarily advocate for any one of the new directions covered, and many others are available beyond the mission and scope of this slim volume. Rather, it critically surveys their key ideas and their potential contributions to the development of new and existing intellectual agendas. By the time the book is published, and very likely during the writing of it, other contributions within the field will have emerged that introduce or reintroduce to MOS some of the emergent strands of Marxist theorising discussed and explored in these pages. In all these respects, this is by no means a definitive or stringently up-to-date account of anything like a 'state of the art'. As a result of reading and teaching the insights of these theoretical tendencies and the different kinds of light they shed on world of work, employment and organisation, it simply gives a flavour of the past, present and future of the application of Marx's CoPE within a delimited disciplinary context, as a basis for further discussion and development.

Of course, the application of the tools of critical social science to the study of management and organisation is by no means novel. Critical management studies (CMS) has become a hegemonic force within MOS today. CMS emerged in the 1980s and the 1990s in Europe under the influence of post-structuralism, among academics in business and management schools seeking to escape the constraints of both mainstream management thinking and orthodox Marxist approaches to the study of work and organisation.[7] Influenced by twentieth-century critical theory, CMS eschews both mainstream and Marxist versions of economic determinism and rationalism in the study of management, as well as rejecting their common assumptions around objective truth, reason and the force of historical progress.

Against the backdrop of the broader 'linguistic turn' in the social sciences inspired by post-structuralism, critically oriented MOS shook off an understanding of power relations rooted in the capital–labour antagonism, stressing instead normative, socio-ideological forms of workplace control and resistance. As CMS questioned the historical materialist emphasis on the economic 'base' over the ideational superstructure, and cast doubt on the conceptualisation of the working class as a privileged social and political actor, Marxism attained an increasingly 'residual' status in MOS more generally, supplanted in the study of work and organisation by other theoretical traditions that foregrounded instead 'practices, techniques, procedures, forms of knowledge and modes of rationality that are routinely deployed in attempts to shape the conducts of others', with particular attention on how workers themselves partake in their own subordination.[8]

Showing how cultural and social dynamics overlay and overdetermine economic imperatives, and emphasising discursive and linguistic processes of power and resistance over material dynamics, CMS has been a valuable corrective to misguided received wisdom from both Marxists and mainstream management scholars. But critics have noted how, whilst this evolution registers the 'political and symbolic dynamics of organizing', it also represents an analytical 'Achilles' heel', eliding how value and exchange relations underpin these dynamics.[9] Whilst doing away with historical materialist determinism and its dualistic ontology of base and superstructure, once the ideational dimension of power is put at centre stage and struggle is reconceptualised as occurring on the plane of subjectivity and identity, value tends to disappear from analyses and critique becomes a synonym of deconstruction and denaturalisation. The social constitution of struggles in a set of materially constituted antagonistic social relations slides from view, along with the expression of these relations in the capitalist social forms—such as value, labour, money, and state—that are the preserve of analyses informed by Marx's CoPE.

Rather than reengaging with Marx's CoPE on this terrain, the discursive turn inaugurated by the advent of CMS paved the way instead for the wider reception within organisational analysis of non-materialist, non-Marxist readings of value such as those associated with the sociology of valuation and evaluation, 'cultural economy' approaches and Actor Network Theory.[10] These approaches have produced a substantial empirical research agenda focused on the role of 'market devices' in discursively constructing value, capturing the social character of value as an economic category and the functioning of markets. But critics argue that these novel approaches to integrating the study of value in MOS insufficiently engage with structural forms of power and the possibility of alternatives, erase human contestation from social change in favour of non-human 'actors', and elide abstract processes of capitalist social mediation such as the extraction of surplus value in the constitution of markets.[11] In theorising and researching value, therefore, such approaches obscure that value is something more than a discursive or technical process associated with neutral non-human assemblages, and disembed its social meaning from political economy.

Beyond the issue of value, CMS has been criticised on a number of other terrains touching upon labour, class and social antagonism. Critics also focus on the political implications of adopting a social constructivist epistemology and a diffuse understanding of power. This approach, it has been argued, dissolves any idea of class relations as a key articulation of power in the workplace.[12] Critics point to how an analytical focus on language and identity has entailed a neglect of material aspects of workplace life and the material outcomes of power inequality.[13] In particular, the issue of the political ineffectiveness of a post-structuralist approach to power has recently emerged as a key concern. Renouncing a priori the possibility of advancing truth claims significantly reduces the political relevance of its scholarship.[14] The CMS community has become increasingly aware of this problem in the post-crisis period, as shown by the internal reflection on its own relevance and 'performativity'.[15] As the world has been beset by profound contemporary challenges and movements for change, CMS's sometimes abstract focus on language and identity over material exploitation and antagonisms has been seen as insufficiently practical and 'performative' outside the narrow confines of academia. In particular, a relativistic approach to objective truth and Enlightenment notions of reason and rationality have been perceived to neuter its political and practical relevance for confronting these challenges and contributing to attempts to change the world of work and wider society.

In focusing on microscopic subjective processes in the workplace, some scholars argue that CMS moves too far from the contextualisation of work within a wider set of economic dynamics—for example, around value creation and capture, profit maximisation, work intensification, imposition of new technologies, exploitation, and property ownership. In response to, and amidst, deep ongoing conflicts about the modalities of how we organise economy and society, MOS scholars have proposed bringing critical theories of work and value 'back to the forefront of critical organizational scholarship' and, in the process, 'get our hands dirty' with Marx's CoPE once again as a potential solution to the impasse.[16] In this spirit, scholars have been sent back to Marx owing to the renewed concern with the relationship between theory and practice within MOS, the shortcomings in the dominant critical approach to MOS, and the underpinning redundancy of mainstream thinking in the face of the grand challenges of our time. As we will see, the CoPE has recently been used to investigate culture and communication, measurement and management, labour struggles and social conflict, skill and technology and diversity.[17] In these analyses, Marxist conceptual foundations allow scholars to theorise the economic compulsions that drive capitalism's most harmful human and ecological consequences, as well as struggles suggestive of social transformation. In particular, scholars have recently argued that to understand the heterogeneous forms taken by social antagonism today, MOS needs to reengage in novel ways with Marx's foundational idea that, under capitalism, all social relations are mediated by value.[18]

In unveiling how value operates as the organising principle of life under capital by socially mediating relations and shaping the subjectivities of those subject to it, the new directions mapped in this book show that recovering Marx's CoPE is in no way a synonym for falling back into the economic reductionism from which CMS rightly sought to escape. The expansive reinterpretation of Marx's CoPE encountered in the chapters that follow moves through labour and through value to their conditions of possibility, along the way linking the wider political economy with everyday practices and processes of work, social conflict, care, violence and environmental ruin. In doing so, the new directions charted in this book offer an important foundation for developing a Marxian MOS research agenda to address multisided social, political and economic antagonisms in the present age.

The chapters that follow critically review the main Marxian traditions already to varying degrees established in MOS—Labour Process Theory (including the alternative posed to 'core' LPT by so-called 'paleo-Marxism') and autonomist Marxism—as well as those that read or apply critical Marxian theory in new ways that chart a future path for the study of management and organisation—open Marxism, Marxist-Feminism, Black Marxism and ecological Marxism. The chapters show how their understandings of labour and value, developing undeveloped insights from Marx's work, shape our ability to see and understand antagonisms at work and in wider society today. Some of these latter approaches are increasingly central in current theoretical and political debates in other fields of the social sciences. However, they are only now gaining wider application in MOS, and promise to grant scholars and practitioners the tools to tackle some of the key issues and challenges of our time. Taken together, these strands point to how value, as the form assumed by work in capitalist society, mediates not only the capital–labour relation but also a wider array of social relations that expands our conceptualisation of class struggle to include a broader variety of social antagonisms not only in the hidden abode of production but also beyond and behind it. As we will see, this opens up a theoretically and politically renewed research agenda in MOS.

Introducing Marx on labour and value

A recurrent focus of the book's treatment of Marx's CoPE is its exposition of the relationship between labour and value. As a 'category of the fundamental social relations that constitute capitalism', Moishe Postone writes, 'value expresses . . . the basic foundation of capitalist production' and thus constitutes for Marx 'the essential core of capitalism'.[19] The reading of Marx that underpins the theoretical perspectives discussed here differs from some orthodox or conventional understandings of Marx. Carrying over from Smith and Ricardo the idea that labour directly inserts value into products in an embodied fashion, what Postone calls 'traditional Marxism' adds a superficially radical veneer to the underlying theoretical framework of classical political economy.[20] Like Smith and Ricardo, this treats the labour process and the sphere of production as ultimately unchanging transhistorical features of any society onto which different kinds of market, property and class relations are imposed. The contradictions of capitalism—inequality, poverty and injustice—are thus seen as relating to the particular form the valorisation process assumes in the contemporary economy, the solution to this typically envisaged as a new, more socialist economy where a different set of class relations would administer essentially the same mode of production. This 'traditional Marxist' approach, Postone argues, adopts the standpoint of the labour process or the 'real economy' to criticise how the value it produces is appropriated and distributed in the market or economy at large by apparently 'non-productive' classes. Where enacted in the 'actually existing' socialist countries of the twentieth century, this resulted in the abolition of the 'liberal bourgeois mode of distribution' and its associated freedoms but retained the same set of production relations under the power of an authoritarian state instead.[21]

Often running contrary to much of the way Marx's work has been received and mediated through the prism of the authoritarian political projects of state socialism and communism, it is in *Capital* that we gain the greatest sense of Marx's CoPE, and where his value theory is outlined in most detail.[22] The dialectical character of the concept of value, and the unfinished and fragmentary character of much of Marx's work on the topic, leaves lasting debates about value theory within the Marxist tradition, including where it influences MOS. Nonetheless, the latest and most cutting-edge scholarship available on Marx's work helps identify several key aspects of his CoPE.[23] In doing so, these readings hark back to a line of scholarship inspired by the dissident Soviet-era intellectual Isaak Rubin, Frankfurt School critical theorists like Alfred Sohn-Rethel and thinkers associated with the *neue Marx-lekture* or 'new reading of Marx'.[24] From this perspective, Marx's CoPE proceeds from a central theoretical issue: why the content of life under capital should assume the forms it does.[25] In this sense, the purpose of Marx's CoPE is not to decode the 'material-technical aspect of the capitalist mode of production', but rather the particular social forms in which it results.[26] Working through the contradictions of the key categories of classical political economy, Marx's method in *Capital* begins from the dominant form in which wealth presents itself to us in capitalist society—as a vast array of commodities, or goods or services produced not to be used but rather to be exchanged for money on the market, and thus bearing monetary value—and then gradually unfolds the social and historical determinants and conditions of this state of affairs.

As Marx shows in the progressive unfolding of these determinations in *Capital*, the historical and logical precondition of this state of affairs rests in the separation of one class from the means of subsisting independent of the sale of their *labour power*—an essential concept in the chapters that follow, indicating not labour itself but the potential capacity to labour when applied to means of production. Meanwhile, the means of production necessary to actualise this potential to labour are concentrated in the hands of another class. Where the former class reproduces itself through selling their labour power, the latter reproduces itself by buying that labour power and consuming it in the 'hidden abode' of production of commodities for exchange in pursuit of expanded value and profit in the market, expressed in money. Meanwhile, those dependent on disposing of the one commodity they own—labour power—live through acquiring commodities on the market with the wage they are paid as the price of that labour power. In this way, these antagonistic social relations generalise money and commodity exchange as the structuring principle not only of production but also of subsistence and thus life itself in capitalist society.

Whilst products of labour in all modes of production might be characterised as having specific and intrinsic 'use' values associated with the function of meeting human needs in this way, commodities in capitalist society are characterised by their *exchange* value—the value that they acquire through the social act of exchange with other such goods or services. It is through this exchange that a commodity acquires value, expressed in money as a general equivalent relating and commensurating heterogeneous goods and services for their specific uses, and, indirectly, their producers. The novelty of Marx's value theory is thus its monetary character, expressed in its explanation of how the concrete individual labour expended in production is 'validated', as a value-producing part of the total abstract labour of society as a whole through the monetary commensuration of its products in exchange.[27]

Breaking with prior classical political economists like Ricardo, and contrary to the common understanding of Marx's theory of value as a '*labour* theory of value', Marx's CoPE as presented in *Capital* refutes a direct causal relation between 'mutually independent acts of [concrete] labour, performed in isolation by individuals', and the production of value.[28] Concrete labour expended in production, from this perspective, produces not value but the specific useful goods or service that carries the *potentiality* to become a commodity and thus to establish a social relation between things upon exchange. Value is thus attributed not to individual commodities but rather to their relation with all the other commodities traded on the market by means of monetary exchange: it is the social form things acquire in capitalist exchange.[29]

It is only through the abstraction of heterogeneous concrete acts of labour as commensurate and equivalent in the successful exchange of their products that they are retrospectively validated as productive of value.[30] It is a social mediation established between production processes after the fact. For Marx, exchange validates whether the labour expended conforms to prevailing standards of 'social necessity'. In this way, 'socially necessary labour time' (SNLT) is determined by, as Marx writes, 'the conditions of production normal for a given society and with the average degree of skill and intensity of labour prevalent in that society'.[31] What is 'average' here is arbitrated by the market. The monetary exchange of its products socially validates labour's conformity with the average 'time taken' for the production of goods and services according to 'monetary social demand' which, imposed upon the labour process, compels concrete labour to 'occur within the time of its abstract measure'—SNLT.[32] That is, exchange validates whether the good was ushered to market in the time and in quantity and quality sufficient to ensure the continuation of the specific capitalist enterprise in competition with all others. To successfully achieve social validation, concrete labour must conform to standards of social necessity 'under average conditions' of production, be expended in line with the 'monetary social demand' in the market for its specific use-values, and reflect the level of skill associated in society with the type of worker carrying it out in production.[33] It is in the market that money 'constructs the social coordination of private labour', establishing in exchange the fullest socialisation of labour.[34]

In production itself, then, 'the value of things' is only 'considered' in an ideal and preemptory sense through labour's 'practical abstraction' in frameworks of measurement and quantification.[35] It is impossible for firms to 'determine prior to actual exchange' whether the immediate concrete labour expended in production will be validated in line with prevailing standards of social necessity.[36] Thus, the individual expenditure and experience of concrete wage labour in production are measured in the workplace through standards and expectations set outside production itself, in the market and in society at large, determined by demand, regulation, competition and other factors, before social validation in the market. By conceptualising value as emerging in market exchange, Marx thus opens a path to the understanding of class struggles as surrounding the social validation of labour, re-embedding the modalities of measurement and control inside and outside the workplace into a wider process of capitalist valorisation.

Whilst a rich source of theoretical reflection around the conceptualisation of contemporary work and economic life, this theory of value functions at a level of such abstraction that the empirical application of its analysis of the 'non-empirical reality' of value as a social form in programmes of social and workplace research would appear to be somewhat limited.[37] However, as Marx's theoretical edifice was left unfinished and fragmentary, the imperative falls upon his readers to reconstruct the full ramifications of his value theory in directions that can suit different empirical purposes.[38] As an unfinished work, *Capital* gives tantalising glimpses of the application of the analysis of social form to other areas, such as the state. In this way, and contrary to approaches that prioritise historical materialism as a kind of economic determinism, we can thus understand Marx's CoPE as an expansive 'theory of historically specific social mediation' for which market mediation operates as a totalising *organising principle* of life, shaping the subjectivities of not only workers but also all social actors.[39]

In this way, the Marxian theories encountered in this book share an understanding of labour and value as forms social relations assume under capitalism, and therefore hardwired with, and into, societal antagonism. Value is here not an immaterial discursive or ideological process of mediation. It articulates the social and the material in ways that are productive of specific relations of exploitation, oppression and subordination and classed, racialised and gendered subjectivities which constitute the terrain on which capitalism's contradictions become visible and antagonisms take place. But, as a 'real' abstraction that exists between things, value cannot simply be replaced through practical projects of transformative social change or radical experimentation. Nor can it be overcome by workers gaining control of the process of capitalist valorisation if the latter is left unchanged. Capitalist value needs to be confronted through the social processes that constitute and concretise it in and through processes of production, circulation and social reproduction. As we will see, this gestures towards a wide array of struggles and an expansive search for alternative forms of remediating social relations.

The structure of this book: into, beyond and behind the hidden abode

In *Capital*, Marx begins with the 'theological niceties' of value and the commodity form to progressively unfold their determinations first through his dive into the 'hidden abode of production' and then, as his critique continues, into the determinations of wage labour in historical processes of dispossession and appropriation. Hence, Marx ends his masterwork by uncovering the 'primitive accumulation' in which capitalist social relations are established. This is not only a historical condition but also an ongoing aspect of the social constitution of capitalist society. The separation of one group of human subjects from the independent individual or collective means of sustaining themselves and others, and the accrual of those means in the hands of another, is continually reinforced as a guarantee of the social relations and social forms associated with value. Peeling back the layers in this way, Marx shows that, in order to understand how society works, and lay bare its organisation around the pursuit of a surplus, we need to delve not only into the sphere of production but also beyond and behind it. Not only is human labour shaped by the overall 'valorisation process' but also is made possible historically and continuingly in a whole set of other classed, gendered, racialised and ecological relationships. Resting beyond and behind the 'hidden abode' of production, these play a role in reproducing the conditions of labour power.[40]

It is this movement into, beyond and behind the hidden abode that this book traces. In Chapter 2, we delve *into* the hidden abode by means of LPT and the analysis it offers of how labour shapes and is shaped by the valorisation process. It connects the key elements of 'core' LPT to concepts and debates within Marxian value theory, specifically with regard to the contingent association between what happens in the workplace and what happens in the market and broader sphere of social and political conflict. It gives an empirical illustration of how LPT scholars have sought to address the category of value in programmes of research about the creative industries and financialisation, before considering the potential alternative posed to 'core' LPT by so-called 'paleo-Marxism' and its appraisal of the possibility for technological transformations and management techniques to challenge capitalist social relations.

LPT in turn provides a basis for combination with other complementary perspectives on wider moments of a broader social totality. Pushing beyond the 'hidden abode' of production, Chapter 3 introduces autonomist Marxism, principally through the prism of the reception within studies of management and organisation of Italian theoretical traditions of workerism and post-workerism (or *operaismo* and *postoperaismo*). The chapter first outlines the history of the development of workerist thought focused on class struggle mainly residing in the factory into post-workerist thought fully engaged with struggles in the wider 'social factory' afforded by changes in the organisation of capitalist production. It then surveys the uptake within MOS of ideas around 'immaterial labour' and the crisis of measurement and value this is said to spark in contemporary capitalism. It then considers, and critiques, a series of autonomist approaches within MOS that remain closer to original 'workerism' insofar as they maintain the relevance of sci-entific management methods in an age of 'digital Taylorism' and emphasise how processes of class composition continue to mediate between the work-place and wider society.

Peering behind the 'hidden abode' of production to uncover the histori-cal and material conditions that underpin it, Chapter 4 introduces four new directions in the application of Marx's CoPE, which together explore issues like class, race and gender, not as isolated instances but intersectionally intertwined aspects of the totality of capitalist social relations. Critically developing the incomplete insights provided by autonomist Marxism, first, the chapter surveys open Marxism's analysis of the constitution of capital-ist society in antagonistic social relations centred on the dispossession of one class from the means of subsistence, mediated by the state. Second, it evaluates how Marxist-Feminist theories of social reproduction understand the relationship between gender divisions of labour and the reproduction of labour power, drawing on an empirical case study of the platform economy. Third, it considers Black Marxism's contribution to the understanding of capitalism's constitution in processes of primitive accumulation and racial domination, illustrated with the example of how industrial change and incar-ceration intertwine for racialised 'surplus populations' in the United States. The chapter relates this analysis of antiblackness to the critical Marxist account of antisemitism as a truncated critique of capitalist social relations. Fourth, the chapter uses ecological Marxism to situate the environmental crisis in labour's 'social metabolism' with nature, drawing upon a case study of labour in the so-called 'circular economy'. Engaging key Marxian concepts with the climate crisis, this highlights how, through the intrinsic human metabolism with nature that our alienated productive activity repre-sents, society has exhausted the capacity of nature to keep on furnishing us with the raw materials necessary to subsist and survive.

With the exception of the foundations provided by LPT and aspects of autonomist Marxism, the approaches surveyed here have remained to date largely underused in MOS despite their centrality in current theoretical and political debates in other fields of the social sciences. The chapters that follow discuss how they distinctively conceptualise the relationship between labour and value and expand our understanding of class struggles and antagonisms. For each approach covered here, empirical illustrations are provided from across a wide range of societal and industrial settings. The final chapter— the Conclusion—considers alternatives and the role a Marxian MOS can play in envisioning them, reflecting on the overall potential of these per-spectives for broadening and renewing critically oriented MOS towards the politics and political economy of value and work in capitalist society.

As we will see, approaches drawing upon the CoPE, such as those charted in this book, enable us to think through how value, as a social and economic category, is conceived of politically; the implications for the politics of work and its futures; and the consequences of different perspectives on value for the production of policy around work, employment and economic life more broadly. Reconnecting with the account of post-crisis 'productivist' approaches to the connection between labour and value given in the introductory chapter, the chapter considers how the radical imaginary of alternatives to contemporary capitalism has been driven by a parallel 'distributionist' orientation to policymaking. Holding the problem with capitalism to be abstract market forces imposed upon an otherwise pure 'real economy' of commodity production, the solution is often addressed to redistributing the proceeds of growth rather than fundamentally challenging the relations under which wealth is produced to begin with. The theoretical approaches developed in previous chapters, which place a joint focus on both concrete and abstract, subjective and objective, and political and economic aspects of the labour process and valorisation process together, are taken to provide the basis for new struggles over recognition and revaluation of value that connect with the politics of power, control and identity central to contemporary societal and ideological conflicts.

In sum, the new and existing approaches we encounter over the course of these chapters expose economic categories like value not just as discursive, abstract rhetorical constructions or expressions of false consciousness, but rather as concretely grounded in an articulation of the social and the material. There are abstractions active in the world around us that, whilst sometimes fleeting and ephemeral, have a real impact and force. Even a category as seemingly immaterial and mysterious as value structures the way that work is performed and experienced, the way that we understand and dispose of the money in our pockets and the way we consume the goods it acquires—in other ways, how we reproduce our conditions of living as human beings. By bringing to light this articulation of the social and material, the perspectives covered here each in their own way perform the vital role of critical theory in unpacking economic categories and exposing their performative social and political content, whilst also revealing the constitution of these social and political categories in material and economic processes and vice versa. In doing so, they open up new directions of critical inquiry for MOS, developing Marx's CoPE not as an argument for the 'primacy of the economic', but rather one that concerns the 'social production and reproduction of the life of society as a whole', opening out upon historically specific forms of capitalist society that 'are pervasive and of great consequence', reaching 'all the way down' into how the things we need to live are produced and how we attain them.[41] In distinct yet mutually compatible ways, the new directions surveyed here also reconnect commodified labour to the wider circuit of capital mediating social relations in the workplace and the life-world more broadly. They thus offer a conceptualisation of value that avoids taking value at 'face value', as do mainstream approaches that disconnect value from labour and its forms of mediation.

***

This book, whilst short and introductory, represents the condensation of bits and pieces of work completed over the course of what is now 5 or 6 years. Within the tumult of that half decade or more, my own valuation of the merits of Marx(ism) and the clunky term 'management and organisation studies' has fluctuated according to the limits of their political and academic mediation in the context of a series of crises both global and local. But there is still much to be learnt, if not from Marxists themselves, then from the creative purposes to which elements of Marx's unfinished work are being put by heterodox social scientists and critical theorists, not to mention activists and social movements, and this can undoubtedly enrich the study of organisations and organising within and without the world of management and business schools.

This volume was written at the prompting of Terry Clague at Routledge, who is warmly thanked for his encouragement many years ago that what was at one point an unpublishably long journal paper might in fact better make a book. Brought together as the COVID-19 pandemic raged, the chapters themselves were finalised in the form of lectures and draft materials shared and discussed with postgraduate students on the 'Work in Capitalist Society' unit I teach in the School of Management at University of Bristol—thanks to all involved. As the book's form and content have changed so much over the last half a decade, it would be unfair to implicate directly the many friends, colleagues and anonymous reviewers who have read and commented on its various iterations and elements, but they (may) know who they are and are warmly thanked. The manuscript has also benefitted, in its manifold earlier guises, from feedback at presentations in a number of streams and panels at conferences over the years. My thanks to all involved in convening and facilitating these opportunities to share the work in progress. Finally, and most importantly, the book could not have come about without the inspiration of a long collaboration and correspondence with Patrizia Zanoni about Marxism and MOS. Massive thanks to Patrizia, and to Hasselt University for the Incoming Mobility Grant that kick-started our conversation. Needless to say, all the usual disclaimers apply, and all errors are mine alone!

Notes

1 Carney M (2020) How we get what we value: The BBC Reith lectures 2020. Available at: www.bbc.co.uk/programmes/m000py8t
2 Carney M (2020) *Value(s)*. London: William Collins.
3 Mazzucato M (2019) *The Value of Everything*. London: Penguin.
4 Mirowski P (1989) *More Heat Than Light: Economics as Social Physics, Physics as Nature's Economics*. Cambridge: Cambridge University Press.
5 Pitts FH (2020) *Value*. Cambridge: Polity.
6 Muller JW (2016) *What Is Populism?* Pittsburgh: University of Pennsylvania Press.
7 Alvesson M, Willmott H (eds.) (1992) *Critical Management Studies*. London: Sage.
8 Knights D, Vurdubakis T (1994) Foucault, power, resistance and all that. In: *Resistance and Power in Organizations*. London: Routledge, 167–198; Parker M (2005) Writing critical management studies. In: Grey C, Willmott H (eds.) *Critical Management Studies: A Reader*. Oxford: Oxford University Press, pp. 353–363; Knights D, Willmott H (1989) Power and subjectivity at work. *Sociology* 23: 535–558; Adler P, Forbes LC, Willmott H (2007) Critical management studies. *Academy of Management Annals* 1(1): 119–179.
9 Prichard C, Mir R (2010) Organizing value. *Organization* 17(5): 507–515 (510).
10 Callon M, Muniesa F (2005) Economic markets as calculative collective devices. *Organization Studies* 26(8): 1229–1250; Beunza D, Hardie I, MacKenzie D (2006) A price is a social thing. *Organization Studies* 27(5): 721–745
11 Fine B (2003) Callonistics. *Economy and Society* 32(3): 478–484; Whittle A, Spicer A (2008) Is actor network theory critique? *Organization Studies* 29(4): 611–629; Roberts JM (2012) Poststructuralism against poststructuralism. *European Journal of Social Theory* 15(1): 35–53.
12 Reed M (2000) The limits of discourse analysis in organizational analysis. *Organization* 7: 524–530; Thompson P (1993) Postmodernism: Fatal distraction. In: Hassard J, Marker M (eds.) *Postmodernism and Organizations*. London: Sage; Newton T (1998) Theorizing subjectivity in organizations. *Organization Studies* 19: 415–447.
13 Prichard & Mir 2010.
14 Reed 2000; Thompson 1993; Newton 1998.
15 Spicer A, Alvesson M, Kärreman D (2009) Critical performativity. *Human Relations* 62(4): 537–560; Zanoni P, Contu A, Healy S, Mir R (2017) Post-capitalistic politics in the making. *Organization* 24(5): 575–588; Adler P (2007) The future of critical management studies. *Organization Studies* 28(9): 1313–1345.
16 Prichard & Mir 2010: 511.
17 Böhm S, Land C (2009) No measure for culture? *Capital & Class* 97: 75–98; Böhm S, Land C (2012) The new 'hidden abode'. *Sociological Review* 60(2): 217–240; Beverungen A, Böhm S, Land C (2015) Free labour, social media, management. *Organization Studies* 36(4): 473–489; Harvie D, Milburn K (2010) How organizations value and how value organizes. *Organization* 17(5): 631–636; Adler 2007; Adler P (2009) Marx and organization studies today. In: *Oxford Handbook of Sociology and Organization Studies*. Oxford: Oxford University Press, 62–91; Vidal M, Adler P, Delbridge R (2015) When organization studies turns to societal problems. *Organization Studies* 36(4): 405–422;

Pitts FH (2020a) Measuring and managing creative labour. *Organization.* doi:10.1177/1350508420968187.

18 Prichard & Mir 2010.

19 Postone M (1993) *Time, Labor, and Social Domination.* Cambridge: University Press, 25–26.

20 Postone 1993: 6

21 Postone 1993: 39–40, 64–65.

22 Marx K (1976) *Capital.* Vol. 1. London: Penguin.

23 Pitts FH (2017) *Critiquing Capitalism Today.* New York: Palgrave; Heinrich M (2012) *An Introduction to the Three Volumes of Karl Marx's Capital.* New York: Monthly Review Press.

24 Backhaus HG (1980) On the dialectics of the value-form. *Thesis Eleven* 1: 94–119; Rubin II (1972) *Essays on Marx's Theory of Value.* Unknown: Black and Red; Sohn-Rethel A (1978) *Intellectual and Manual Labour.* London: Macmillan.

25 Marx 1976: 173–174; Bonefeld W (2014) *Critical Theory and the Critique of Political Economy.* London: Bloomsbury, 58.

26 Rubin 1972: 2; Backhaus 1980.

27 Heinrich M, Wei X (2012) The interpretation of capital. *World Review of Political Economy* 2(4): 708–728 (725).

28 Marx 1976: 131.

29 Heinrich M (2017) 'Capital' After MEGA: Discontinuities, interruptions, and new beginnings. *Crisis and Critique* 3(3): 93–138 (126).

30 Heinrich & Wei 2012: 727.

31 Marx 1976: 129.

32 Arthur C (2013) The practical truth of abstract labour. In: Bellofiore R, Starosta G, Thomas P (eds.) *In Marx's Laboratory.* Leiden: Brill, pp. 101–120; Heinrich 2012: 51; Bonefeld W (2010) Abstract labour: Against its nature and on its time. *Capital & Class* 34(2): 257–276 (266–267).

33 Heinrich 2012: 51–52; Marx 1976: 202.

34 Bellofiore R, Riva TR (2015) The Neue Marx-Lektüre. *Radical Philosophy* 189: 24–36 (29).

35 Heinrich 2012: 126; Marx 1976: 128; Arthur 2013.

36 Bellofiore & Riva 2015: 31.

37 Pitts FH (2014) Follow the money? *Ephemera: Theory & Politics in Organization* 14(3): 335–356.

38 Heinrich 2017: 136; Backhaus 1980: 100.

39 Postone M, Brennan T (2009) Labor and the logic of abstraction. *South Atlantic Quarterly* 108(2): 305–330 (310); Backhaus 1980.

40 Fraser N (2014) Behind Marx's hidden abode. *New Left Review* 86: 55–60.

41 Adorno TW (2000) *Introduction to Sociology.* Cambridge: Polity Press; Murray P (2013) Unavoidable crises: Reflections on backhaus and the development of Marx's value-form theory in the *Grundrisse.* In: Bellofiore R, Starosta G, Thomas P (eds.) *In Marx's Laboratory.* Leiden: Brill, pp. 121–146.

2 Into the hidden abode

From the labour process to the valorisation process

Introduction

This chapter establishes foundations for those that follow by considering the relationship between labour, value and class struggles through
the prism of Labour Process Theory (LPT). LPT is the longest standing
approach applying aspects of Marx's critique of political economy (CoPE)
to analyse organisational life. LPT was developed in the late 1970s and
early 1980s; its key thinkers include Harry Braverman, Michael Burawoy,
Richard Edwards, Paul Edwards, Andrew Friedman, Chris Smith and Paul
Thompson.[1] LPT began as an attempt to link labour and class struggle to
their wider political economic context by conceptualising structural conflict in and over the labour process as part and parcel of wider trends in
capitalist accumulation. Independent of changes in what is produced and
how, LPT understands the labour process as both a 'purposeful activity in
which a natural object or raw material is transformed into a useful product
which satisfies a human need', and also, under capitalism, a conversion
of labour power, as the capacity to labour, into labour itself in order to
produce a good bearing both use and, crucially, *exchange* value.[2] Early
proponents explained changes in the workplace as resulting from broader
shifts in the circuit of capital over time through the examination of the
deskilling of labour under monopoly conditions, and the changing relationship between capital, labour and the state.[3]

In the United Kingdom, LPT took its primary inspiration from Braverman's *Labor and Monopoly Capital*, which analysed through a sociological
lens his own experience of factory work to stress the role of capitalist control in shaping the contemporary workplace.[4] In analysing how 'knowledge
is systematically removed from direct producers and concentrated in the
hands of management and their agents' in the capitalist labour process,
Braverman and subsequent scholars saw, in the latter, a tendency towards
the deskilling and degradation of work.[5] 'Post-Bravermanian' LPT,

DOI: 10.4324/9781003198895-2

meanwhile, set out to distance the development of the approach from the remnants of orthodox Marxism that had characterised Braverman's work. These include a failure to reckon with the agency of worker resistance to compel capitalist development; and an overly reductive and one-sidedly downbeat appraisal of both the homogenisation of labour and the different forms control could take in the capitalist labour process. Pushing past these limitations, the resulting 'second-wave' of LPT drew upon heterodox Marxist and non-Marxist sources—including, at its inception, elements of the autonomist thought discussed in the next chapter—to stress the role of worker militancy in shaping the way that management techniques develop within the dialectical tension between resistance and control and within the context of the overarching valorisation process. However, critics have argued that the development of so-called 'core' LPT as an internal critique of its blueprint in Braverman's work unduly discards the latter's 'class analysis' and commitment to socialist transformation for what some characterise as a more 'conservative' and reformist approach. Post-Braverman LPT, on this account, 'coalesced into a new orthodoxy' stripped of any relationship to these revolutionary foundations, their 'origins in Marxism', and their 'radical political implications'.[6]

At its 'core', LPT comprises four key elements, each of which carries over or exists in conversation with aspects of the CoPE: the centrality and relative autonomy of the labour process; the relationship between the valorisation process and the labour process; the imperative of managerial control; and the structured character of the capital–labour antagonism. These flow from the essential point that labour power—'the capacity to work which is transformed into *labour* that produces value for the capitalist through the creation of commodities'—is ultimately indeterminate, as the efficacy and productivity of its expenditure in the production process cannot be 'fixed' in advance and, being part of the 'person of the worker', is embodied according to 'gender, age, nationality, skill, region etc' and thus highly variable.[7] The potential to labour can only be actualised through its application to the means of production, through which labour power is transformed into concrete labour. But because labour power is embodied in human subjects who are not uniform and passive but differentiated and possessed of agency and autonomy, capital struggles to render the consumption of labour power more determinate through the control of workers by management in line with prevailing standards of production enforced by competitive pressures.[8] As what Marx called 'variable capital', then, indeterminate labour power must thus be controlled—through coercion or consent—in order to realise its value to the capitalist. Based on the definition given by Thompson, we will discuss in detail the four key principles that flow from this core insight.

The centrality, and relative autonomy, of labour

Work, as the human metabolism with nature, is mediated as wage labour in capitalist society. Following most mainstream readings of Marx's CoPE, the first core component of LPT is the centrality of the labour process, as the location where the capacity to labour—*labour power*—is actualised as concrete labour, capital is transformed into useful and desirable things, and a surplus generated.[9] As 'a central part of man's experience in acting on the world and reproducing the economy', for LPT, labour possesses 'a privileged insight' as regards any 'theoretical or political challenge to the system'.[10]

Whilst the labour process plays a vital part in meeting the 'fundamental material and social needs of human life', its specificity in capitalist society is that it produces things not simply for use but for exchange. Moreover, in capitalist society, this is not an end in itself, but conducted for the purposes of generating a profit, and valorising invested value, through the production and circulation of commodified goods and services. Precapitalist labour processes were not mediated primarily by the pursuit of profit and the expansion of invested value as the golden cord connecting all human life. In capitalist society, where growth undergirds nearly every aspect of social, political and economic life, human productive activity produces more than this, generating 'a world of appearances'. These include social forms and social relations encompassing 'ownership, control . . . power and knowledge' that stand apart from human subjects even whilst springing from their creative actions.[11] As human subjectivity objectified in an external reality, our work disappears into a world it helps make and remake, with 'social relations involving people . . . represented as relations between unalterable *things*'.[12] This carries over Marx's understanding of fetishism outlined in *Capital*. In particular, this acceptance of a cornerstone concept of the CoPE and subsequent critical theory influences LPT's reading of technology not as a neutral outcome of innovation or human problem-solving but as a product of human work shaped by social purposes that, in capitalist society, are comprehensively reshaped in line with the pursuit of profit, and the imperative of control this implies. Its social constitution grants technology a path dependency in how it is deployed in the workplace and limits the capacity for its recuperation. Technology, as with other aspects of the world of things, is a product of the central role played by human work that turns around to dominate its producers according to the historically specific social relations from which it arises.

Whilst the centrality of labour as a core principle would appear to resonate with many established readings of Marx's CoPE, and its framing through the concept of fetishism reproduces one of Marx's most scintillating insights, critics have nonetheless argued that LPT strays too far from Marx by eliding or ignoring wider 'forms of domination through which labour is subjugated to capital'.[13] From a Marxist perspective, there has also been criticism of the way in which LPT apparently liquidates wider political and social conflict as a site of analytical significance, eliding both extra-workplace expressions of class struggle and contestation at the level of the state.[14] However, the centrality of labour carries an important caveat, insofar as labour has no 'specific significance for analysing other social relations outside production' and possesses a 'relative autonomy' from 'external forces and influences' specific to 'other spheres of social life'.[15] Outside phenomena are mediated according to the particular characteristics of the labour process just as the labour process is mediated by its social, political and economic context. In this way, LPT makes no claim to be a totalising theory that imposes its unit of analysis—the labour process—onto every other aspect of society. Rather, it provides a basis for development and extension with reference to other ideas and theories that, in combination with LPT, can enable a broader frame of reference for the analysis of other moments of the social totality.

This movement between the labour process and its mediation of wider social relations exposes the salience of subjectivity to the study of the labour process as something more than the rational 'production of profitable goods and services'. A purely rational and economistic explanation cannot capture why, for instance, 'workers get attached to routines that are seemingly devoid of self-expression'.[16] Accounting for the creativity of capital in organising the labour process to ensure exploitation in spite of long-term macro-scale tendencies of capitalist reproduction, Burawoy's seminal insights on the elicitation of workers' consent powered a second wave of labour process analysis that built upon LPT's understanding of the centrality of antagonism to capitalist development to reinstate culture and subjectivity in the study of processes of control and resistance.[17] LPT would also later spawn a breakaway strand of Critical Management Studies (CMS) out of dissatisfaction with its existing attempts to describe and analyse this subjective element of labour.[18]

Whilst the labour process undoubtedly occupies an ontologically and epistemologically important perspective in the analysis of the workings of capitalism for LPT, then, the latter does not necessarily emphasise work or workers as the centre of broader social and political conflict or transformation. Contrary to most conventional readings of these categories through a Marxist lens, 'core' LPT distinguishes 'between capital and labour as workplace and societal actors'.[19] In this, it does not carry over from orthodox Marxism a deterministic approach to the relationship between material shifts and processes of class identification. This divergence stems from the

broader observation that many quarters of the Marxist tradition have generally 'failed to present a convincing analysis of the . . . relationship between
class struggle at the level of the factory and class struggle at the level of
society as a whole'.[20] This failure owes to the 'empirically unsustainable
link' Marxists tend to posit between politics at the 'point of production'
and a wider politics of social transformation.[21] Indeed, second-wave LPT's
downbeat appraisal of the possibilities of revolutionary transformation as
dictated in the Marxist 'gravedigger thesis', whereby the objective conditions of capitalism would inevitably produce a revolutionary working class
which would overthrow capitalism, was pivotal in the early distancing of
post-Braverman LPT from orthodox Marxism.[22]

Because there is 'no consistent evidence that the capitalist labour
process . . . create[s] a class identity' of the kind many Marxists have historically anticipated, the more advanced among the latter—like the autonomists
we encounter in the next chapter—have tended to 'displace' the question of
'social transformation' onto 'different terrain[s] of analysis', whether 'different revolutionary subjects'—like youths or students—or 'superstructural
spheres'—like education or consumption, for instance.[23] Whilst refusing to
wish the working class 'farewell' for an equally flawed cause celebre, LPT
abandons this search for a revolutionary working class or a surrogate for it.
In doing so, it theoretically 'reduces the burden on the working class' represented by its ascribed 'mission of emancipating the whole of humanity', for
an understanding 'appropriate to its real rather than imagined intervention
in history'.[24]

In this sense, for LPT, 'there are simply no necessary theoretical or
empirical links between conflict and exploitation at work and . . . wider
social transformations', and no intrinsic or inevitable relationship between
the politics of production and politics in wider society, up to and including
any revolutionary capacity specific to workers.[25] For LPT, the politics of
production have a relative autonomy from material and economic determinants, and are shaped in interaction with a much broader 'totality of social
relations' beyond the workplace. In turn, relations at the point of production do not necessarily determine broader-scale class politics, which
themselves rest on much more diverse and complicated 'complexes of
social practices' irreducible to the relationship between the economic and
the political.[26]

In this way, struggles in the workplace do not directly structure the character of wider class politics or formal politics, not least because 'different
sections of the working class have different, even antagonistic, interests
whose resolution will be a political question irreducible to the "science"
of "political economy"', and contingent on a host of extraeconomic

conditions.[27] As such core LPT negates the possibility of a 'workerist political theory' such as that encountered in the next chapter, whether directly applied to the working class or through displacement onto new productive subjectivities when the working class fails to do what radicals expect or demand it does. This approach has received criticism for its perceived distance from traditional Marxism and its reformist refusal of a revolutionary approach to collective class struggle.[28] In particular, the reluctance of 'core' LPT to connect the labour process to broader class analysis has led some to criticise a perceived absence of direct strategic relevance for contemporary struggles. LPT analyses of new class strata such as those associated with managerial and professional work tend to see the proliferation of such strata as playing a mediating role with reference to the structural antagonisms that underpin capitalist society, rather than intensifying class conflict by reinforcing one side of the struggle.[29] By including such strata within a heterogeneous but universal working class defined by the broad association with wage labour, critics argue, LPT analyses contribute little to the identification of specific class actors occupying strategically significant positions vis-à-vis the production of surplus-value and wider social antagonisms.

It should nonetheless be noted that LPT is home to scholarship that combines precisely these more radical and revolutionary principles with a focus on control and resistance at the point of production. Indeed, the capacity to do so is afforded by the fact that LPT makes no claim to provide a coherent, totalising class theory that explains how different economic actors behave politically based on interests formed in production, accepting instead that this connection is ultimately contingent and context-specific and thus open to interpretation through different frames.[30]

The labour process and the valorisation process

The second component of 'core' LPT indebted to the critique of political economy is that competition drives capital 'constantly to revolutionise the production process', although the degree of freedom management retains vis-a-vis the imperative of capitalist valorisation has evolved over time, and is contingent on specific circumstances. In this respect, LPT's roots in Marx's CoPE are clear in its understanding of capitalism as 'a mode of production based on the generalised production of commodities for exchange and profit'. Through this prism, LPT considers the labour process as it appears in capitalist society: as 'a framework within which those who own and control the economic resources seek to ensure the appropriation of the surplus'—in other words, in the context of the valorisation process, and the circuit of capital as a whole. The compulsion to constantly expand value as a condition of society's reproduction is, for this perspective, what distinguishes it as 'distinctively capitalist' in the first place. The centrality of the surplus, and the propulsive power of competition that the search for profit compels, decisively differentiate the capitalist labour process from any preexisting simple process of production and exchange, with capitalists, managers and workers alike all subject to its satisfaction.[31]

Despite the inheritance of this standpoint from the CoPE, LPT carries the persistent connotation in the eyes of its critics of failing to account for what Marx called the 'valorisation process'. According to some critics, early on in the development of LPT, there was a tendency to forego any concerted inquiry into the character of value relations in the circuit of capital as a whole owing to the assumption that prevailing monopoly conditions enabled capital to profit from manipulation of product markets alone, freeing managers to experiment with different means of eliciting effort and consent from employees undetermined by the valorisation process whilst also permitting workers 'political space' to intervene in these methods, producing among labour process scholars a sometimes narrow focus on labour alone.[32] From this perspective, whereas the earlier likes of Braverman followed Marx in relating job design and deskilling to the dynamics of capital accumulation, later LPT came to 'hive off—conceptually or analytically—the labour process from the valorisation process'.[33] In particular, critiques of Braverman's 'deskilling thesis' led so-called 'second-wave' LPT to increasingly emphasise the relative autonomy of managerial control from the abstract economic imperatives of capitalist social relations.[34]

In light of this, scholars have criticised LPT for its 'managerialism', granting too much agency to managers relative to the backdrop of the 'the capitalist circuit by which valorization occurs'.[35] For some critics, this relates to a break with classical Marxism and the absence of a conceptualisation of value in the circuit of capital as a whole.[36] Although LPT holds to an understanding of exploitation indebted to Marx, it refutes the traditional labour theory of value in that it posits no direct or necessary relationship between concrete labour and the value of commodities established in exchange.[37] Being seen to have accepted the 'empirical unproveability' of the labour theory of value, early strands of post-Braverman LPT have been considered by critics to have seldom 'considered the labour process from the point of view of value', leaving largely unaddressed the systemic imperatives and structural conditions that drive capitalist accumulation.[38]

In spite of, or perhaps because of, these critiques, second-wave LPT increasingly recognised that a focus on the valorisation process represented a necessary alternative to the orthodox Marxist preoccupation with the capital–labour contradiction at the point of production, and a complement to LPT's tendency to emphasise on managerial control on the shopfloor. Thus, the critiques helped correct a tendency to cleave off questions of the ownership and accumulation of capital, where in fact 'what makes the labour process specifically capitalist is the unity of the process of production with valorisation', rather than anything confined to the labour process itself.[39] However, there are limits to applying a sometimes abstract 'logic of valorisation' to the labour process. For LPT, there is ultimately no inevitable or deterministic relationship between the dynamics of the valorisation process and the contingent decisions of capital to reconfigure the labour process, although the valorisation process may, in certain circumstances, set limits on cost considerations that in turn constrain the capacity to grant workers autonomy and opportunities for creativity, for example. In a trenchant critique, Thompson contended that appeals to the 'logic' of valorisation and its impacts seldom concretely show the empirical 'connections between valorisation, exploitation and control', as they play out both within and beyond the workplace. LPT, meanwhile, contrary to the caricature presented by its critics, retains a sense of production's broader context within the overall process of valorisation by empirically evidencing how the latter compels capital to ensure workplace control—'directing, supervising, evaluating, disciplining and rewarding' labour—in order to turn a profit, against which workers struggle for their own forms of control through unions and other means, themselves playing an active, and not a passive, role in resisting, reproducing and shaping forms of 'work allocation, intensity and reward'.[40] In this way, the labour process, whilst possessing some core characteristics, is shaped and conditioned by the particular forms of state regulation and 'societal and market conditions' that govern the production and appropriation of the surplus in different political and economic contexts.[41]

Inspired by this approach, in recent years, scholars in the tradition have come to adopt a 'full circuit of capital' perspective including both the purchase of labour power and the realisation of value in product markets.[42] In particular, Global Value Chains and Global Production Networks approaches have provided LPT a basis to associate workplace regimes at the level of the labour process with value logics at the level of the circuit of capital on a global scale.[43] Furthermore, the concept of 'value logics' has been deployed to articulate the relation between valorisation, financialisation and the workplace.[44] Of particular interest are LPT studies of the increasingly variegated character of contemporary capitalism and the ascendancy of authoritarian state-capital combinations. Stimulated by a return to

Burawoy's conceptualisation of 'factory regimes', this developing strand of LPT scholarship captures the character of labour conditions and governance in rising economies like China, and the use of the 'varieties of capitalism' literature as a means to reconnect the workplace to a wider comparative view of institutions.[45] This evidences the openness of LPT to combination with other perspectives capable of shedding light on different moments of capitalist valorisation and reproduction.

The imperative of managerial control and structured antagonism

A third, related, point central to core LPT is the imperative of control, which represents 'the primary arena of social relations within all societies in the era of monopoly capitalism'.[46] To begin with, as we have seen, the acquisition of labour power in the labour market makes no guarantee of its efficacy when consumed in production. Moreover, as noted earlier, there is no predetermined symmetry between the conditions for the realisation of value in the valorisation process and the labour expended in the production of the goods and services that bear that value. The latter may vary above or below the standards of productivity and efficiency established in and by the market through competition between capitals. The incapacity of the market alone to determine these outcomes leaves employers and managers responsible for extracting effort in line with prevailing expectations, principally by 'extending workers' time at work' or 'intensifying their productivity within the same time' but more broadly by 'monopolising judgement, knowledge and the conceptual side of the work, and concomitantly excluding workers from control and ownership of knowledge and skill acquisition'.[47]

In line with other parts of the Marxist tradition, LPT focuses on the relationship between forms of control and the resistance that both spring from and drives them. The fact that labour power can only be consumed in production by means of the management of autonomous human agents, possessed of body and mind, renders work an intrinsically 'contested terrain'.[48] In production, this centres on competing claims to control by capital—which must supervise, discipline and measure labour in pursuit of profit—and labour, which must manage the employment relationship in the other direction via unions and other means. With reference to the frameworks through which this 'contested terrain' plays out, the fourth insight 'core' to LPT is, following Paul Edwards, the 'structured' character of the antagonism between capital and labour, whereby the indeterminacy of labour power is worked out through forms of control and resistance, mediated by collective bargaining, that do not necessarily burst out into 'visible conflicts'.[49]

The second wave of LPT examines how, scientific management having proved increasingly ineffective at securing control over workers, managers seek consent and legitimation instead.[50] Unable to depend solely on control through coercion, capital engages and incorporates workers through a range of institutional and cultural techniques for generating cooperation and consent. This is underpinned by the sometimes contradictory material and ideological impulses that bind workers and their social reproduction to the interests of their employers. This mediates both the resistance workers engage in and the forms of control to which they are subject in response.[51] In its classical sense, this competition over control has been governed by a system of industrial relations that accepts workplace conflict as inevitable, seeking to provide channels through which antagonism can play out and through which competing sides can have their voice represented. At a collective and institutional level, this structured antagonism has been mediated by trade unionism, which has as its essence 'the *bargain* between capital and labour over the terms of the sale of labour power'.[52]

At the same time, the increasing association of competitiveness and commitment with greater creativity and freedom at work in the latter part of the late twentieth century was epitomised in the idea of 'responsible autonomy' as an alternative to the 'direct authority' of Taylorism.[53] Whilst scientific management still persisted in some sense, it eventually came to hinge less on deskilling and degradation, and more on 'creative participation' in exchange for commitment to the 'competitive aims of enterprise', not only individually but also collectively through the changing ways that unions perceived their mission. The resulting shifts in workplace relations softened the original position of LPT on the inevitability of the valorisation process pushing capitalists to cheapen, deskill and degrade work. Meeting the requirements of the valorisation process was increasingly seen as resting on a diverse range of tactics on the part of capital, emboldened by vertical integration and monopoly power in product markets that permitted more flexibility and freedom on the part of employers and managers. Whilst constrained at one end by worker resistance and at the other by 'competitive market pressures', this could even include concessions on pay in pursuit of longer-term profitability, seen as stimulating economic growth.[54]

The evolution in the modalities of managerial control showed the absence of any predetermined relationship between the valorisation process and the capital–labour antagonism, with 'control' and 'resistance' relative forces unfolding in a dialectical tension. An example is how the precondition of many of the affordances of the post-war workplace was the tight technical control instituted under Taylorism, in which workers themselves participated. Unions were empowered in playing a part in trying to 'sustain the means of monitoring, modifying and materially benefitting from the large array of measurement techniques that were a necessary part of payment and production methods' under Taylorism, even as management themselves sought to abandon them.[55] By policing the rates of production on assembly lines in keeping with collectively agreed standards, workers through their unions themselves participated in the maintenance of control even as they were subject to it.

Rather than a decisive shift one way or the other, then, a shifting 'frontier of control' is always at stake between these interrelated forces of 'confrontation and accommodation'.[56] Rather than anything intrinsic to the human side of work—enrichment, motivation, etc.—it is more often the valorisation process, via cost pressures, competitive tendencies and product markets, that compels the introduction of managerial innovations like so-called 'human resource management'. These innovations gave LPT a much more complex picture of the dynamic relation of control and resistance, revealing their internally contradictory character, such that workers resisting subordination might simultaneously identify with the interests of their employer.[57] Management—as the extraction of effort in the indeterminate transformation of labour power into labour—increasingly rested on cultural, discursive and ideological tools for ensuring compliance that a traditional Marxist analysis alone would be ill-equipped to comprehend and scrutinise. Workplace resistance played a vital role in these innovations, militancy compelling management to innovate by 'modifying and multiplying the variety of means used to subordinate labour' and guaranteeing control and profitability through stimulating *consent* from workers, rather than simply coercing them.[58] Where management went, LPT followed.

Researching valorisation and the labour process

Tracking these shifts, LPT moved well beyond Braverman's story of deskilling and degradation on the shopfloor, with empirical studies exploring novel technological configurations running from the computer in the 1980s to the fully fledged 'digital workplace'; the place of gender and the body in proliferating forms of affective labour; the emergence of new occupations with the rise of services, the creative industries and knowledge-based professions; and the effect of global economic changes on workplace life, including post-socialist transition and 'Japanisation' in the 1990s and the rise of China today, to name a few.[59] Here, we will discuss in greater detail two areas of enquiry that speak to some of the key issues raised earlier, specifically around the relationship between value and the labour process: the creative industries as a case study of the changing world of work in the 'new economy', and the role of financialisation in shaping workplace life.

LPT has a long track record of expressing scepticism about the succession of apparent paradigm shifts to which work has been said to be subject over previous decades. At the same time, such paradigm shifts have been taken to challenge and confound LPT. Critics have highlighted areas like the digital and creative industries as exemplifying a new economy where value is produced in increasingly dispersed locations, many of which are outside the workplace or formal employment relationship and thus are taken to disrupt the traditional terrain of labour process analysis.[60] Once labour is defined through its location in the workplace and the role of managers is put at centre stage as in LPT, these critics note, forms of value-producing labour and exploitation occurring elsewhere and beyond managerial control tend to remain excluded from the scope of analysis.[61] Such claims of novelty have been resisted in labour process scholarship through its own study of the creative industries, which has acted as a forum for the integration of insights around value and valorisation with the study of the labour process. Reflecting engagements with concepts of value chains and 'value logics', LPT scholarship on the creative industries bridges the study of the labour process and the valorisation process, reconnecting, if only implicitly, key elements of the CoPE. In line with its aversion to talk of 'paradigm shifts', and underpinned by its critique of technologically or generationally deterministic prognoses about the changing world of work and the rise of novel kinds of labour and class subjectivities, LPT has firmly disputed the claim that a 'communism of capital' is forged within creative industries based on the socialisation of the 'commons' of knowledge and creativity—largely through reasoning that the distinctive combination of valorisation process and labour process keeps capitalist dynamics very much alive in the new world of work.[62]

In particular, LPT studies of the creative industries highlight management's continuing capacity to control and discipline labour in the context of an organisational and industrial setting superficially distinct from the Taylorist factories of the past. Whilst recognising the uncomfortable fit of traditional scientific management processes of 'routinisation' and 'deskilling' with the creative industries, LPT has shone a light on how creative labour is just as closely coordinated and organised as any other scientifically managed labour process, with cultural production rationalised 'both at the creative stage and the circulation stage'.[63] In this last respect, these studies observe that 'tensions in the management of creativity are located largely outside the employment relationship' in the market, often imposing themselves in an active struggle 'against the relative autonomy given to creative workers'.[64] The valorisation process—represented in pressures to win work and keep clients in a competitive market—thus actively shapes the conditions of creative labour, driving processes of 'standardisation and specialisation' associated with scientific management.[65] Whilst not always imposed directly by management within the employment relationship itself, the contradictions and tensions nonetheless play out with 'far greater continuity of conditions and concepts' than allowed for in appeals to the novelty of the 'new economy'.[66] Rather than epochal transformations, then, these analyses refocus attention on the articulation of internal workplace dynamics with an external market context, exposing creative industries as a durably 'industrial' site of production recognisable against more traditional forms of work organisation.

Owing to its alleged examination of 'the labor process in abstraction from the valorization of capital', however, LPT has been repeatedly critiqued for an apparent incapacity to conceptually and methodologically deal with the broader political economic shifts in advanced capitalist economies and their impact on the organisation of work.[67] Whether despite or because of such critiques, in recent years, LPT scholars have reconnected their analyses with moments of 'pre-production, reproduction and post-production', including through the study of how value connects the labour process in the context of broader shifts associated with financialisation.[68] This has spurred a series of contributions interrogating how 'value logics' originating outside the point of production structure and constrain managerial agency.[69]

Many mainstream and Marxist analyses of financialisation tend to see its effects on labour as 'collateral damage' as if the two were unconnected, 'risk and instability' imposed upon production only as a 'secondary effect of macro regime-level changes'.[70] But, for LPT, financialisation does not just work *through* its effects on the labour process but comes about itself as a consequence of shifts in production, in a context where industry has been unable to generate the profitability and productivity required for capitalist reproduction in a globalised economy, sending capital elsewhere for returns.[71] Across this terrain, LPT relates financialisation—and thus the valorisation process—to the workplace, exposing how 'the labour process remains a focal point of productivity gains, restructuring and value capture as part of the delivery of targets to shareholders', which in turn shapes how work is organised and performed.[72] Whilst labour is still a central site of value creation and 'financialisation acts in part through value extraction in the labour process', the pursuit of shareholder value in non-financial corporations actively shapes 'the behaviour of firm management' in such a way to create 'negative impacts' on the kind of 'high performance workplace productivity bargains' central to the structured antagonism that characterised capitalist work in the past.[73]

In this respect, financialisation connects to the workplace, because the valuation of assets in the financial markets by investors and shareholders plays out in turn in the way that labour is valued, measured and managed.

As Cushen and Thompson write, 'financial targets must be delivered by employees', as 'speculative financialised firm valuations' meet a 'moment of truth'. As a consequence of these imperatives, labour costs are squeezed, work is intensified and rendered insecure through processes of 'perpetual restructuring', and 'punitive performance regimes' are introduced in pursuit of short-term quantitative goals servicing targets and valuations set by shareholders and investors. In this last respect, effort is extracted from workers through a vast array of new kinds of measurement and monitoring as market discipline cascades downwards, creating incentives that distort commitment and the collective, collaborative side of working life. As such, 'far from being marginalised by financialisation', the labour process and the employment relationship constitute a key terrain on which financialising tendencies and their tensions play out.[74] These financialised 'value logics' also cascade down through the labour process due to procurement and supply chains, where contractors are subject to measures of 'value-based controls' from lead firms.[75] This is because 'financialisation encouraged the adoption of metric-based calculation in supply chain relations in alignment with the formal rationality and mechanistic evaluation of closed criteria preferred by investors and fund managers'.[76]

In this way, the 'meso-level mechanisms' through which LPT connects the labour process with financialisation can also be used to relate it to other closely associated processes that today interest critical social scientists, such as the study of rentierisation encountered within the work of the autonomists discussed in the next chapter, offering an alternative way to understand the risk and precariousness produced by these tendencies. What Thompson calls 'disconnected capitalism' sees management imperatives around the extraction of 'discretionary effort' reshaped by financialised value logics and entering into conflict with the greater disposability and burden of risk imposed upon workers, with distrust 'undermining the stability and reciprocity necessary for local high performance work system "bargains"' and the kinds of mutual gain strategies they make possible. Whilst shopfloor dynamics express labour's specific vulnerability to 'managerial requirements to service debt, interest payments and higher than average returns over a short time period', this vulnerability is also expressed in a variety of ways beyond the immediate management of the labour process itself, 'through additional risks of job destruction, value transfers from worker wages, pensions and benefits, and work intensification'. The greater disposability of firm assets this induces leads to perpetual restructuring via 'delayering, divestment, disaggregation or downsizing', with workers themselves on the frontline of these changes.[77]

This analysis highlights the danger in attempting to displace the critique of the relationship between the valorisation process and the labour process towards new terrain in the belief that labour no longer really matters to the big political-economic shifts of our time. As Cushen and Thompson comment,

> The expansion of the commodity form and the role of the household in the restructuring of risk, debt and labor are important developments. However, a focus on value extraction beyond the labor process has too often led to a displacement perspective and a paucity of research on the relations between financialisation and the point of production.

It is thus 'necessary to confront perceptions that financialisation has marginalised labor as a source of value due to the proportionate size and influence of the financial sector and financial engineering'. This displacement exercise elides how large non-financial corporations 'are not only increasingly subject to shareholder value pressures through capital markets' but also are themselves 'active players in those processes through markets for corporate control and leveraging value from financial assets'.[78] For LPT, then, financialisation has thus brought to light formerly opaque but nonetheless fundamental processes linking labour and valorisation.

Paleo-Marxism: an alternative to 'core' LPT?

Whilst it accepts that the capitalist labour process has a tendency towards 'fragmentation and mechanization', eroding 'skill and specialized knowledge', for LPT, the centrality of human labour in social production implies that 'workers' skills and creative capacities can never be altogether eliminated from the production process', regardless of apparent technological threats to their preservation.[79] This aligns with a general scepticism within the LPT tradition vis-à-vis claims of imminent ruptures in the world of work and economic life, shored up by considerable body of research providing an alternative to the flimsy empirical basis of contemporary predictions around the automation of work, and reaffirming the meaning of work in the face of its purported crisis.[80]

This pessimistic appraisal of technologically mediated workplace transformations comes down to an understanding of what in Marxist terminology is known as the relationship between the *forces* and *relations* of production, or in other words, the 'distinction between skills, machinery and other physical properties of production, and the social relations of ownership, command and control'.[81] For LPT scholars, these 'act constantly on one another', with the relations taking priority in shaping the forces. This challenges analyses and ideologies that treat science and technology as if they were neutral, autonomously unfolding phenomena to which social relations cannot but adjust. Importantly, it challenges traditional Marxist approaches that see technological advances inevitably bursting through and transforming ossified, outdated social relations on the path to communism. The implication of LPT's stress on the relations of production is that the valorisation process, via financial imperatives, market conditions and ownership models, impacts upon decisions to invest in new technologies such that their availability need not necessarily imply uptake at the level of the labour process in the way prevailing utopian and dystopian expectations anticipate.[82]

Not all sides of the labour process debate have taken such a circumspect view of technology and work, however. One strand, sometimes termed 'paleo-Marxism', represents what might be called a 'techno-determinist' alternative to core LPT, as part of a wider solution proposed to the impasse of CMS.[83] The term 'paleo-Marxism', according to Paul Adler, its chief proponent, is used to differentiate itself from the so-called 'neo-Marxism' of second-wave LPT.[84] Paleo-Marxism is characterised by its application to the study of organisations a traditional understanding of Marx's historical materialist method.[85] Against the technological pessimism of LPT, it pledges to 'restore the causal weight of technology' through an alternative reading of Marx's account of the dialectical relationship between the forces of production—'technology, materials and workers' productive faculties'— and relations of production—'the relations of ownership and control over these productive forces'.[86] For paleo-Marxists, 'core' LPT displaced attention on the technological forces for a narrow focus on the social relations of production. Paleo-Marxism, meanwhile, sees the forces of production as the moving principle of capitalist development, to which the relations of production stand as fetters and to which management practices and social organisation must adapt. Paleo-Marxism thus presents itself as an attempt to 'restore to prominence Marxian value theory' that had been displaced by LPT's focus on the relations of production through the conceptual rehousing of the labour process within wider dynamics of capitalist valorisation.[87]

The dialectical relationship between the forces and the relations of production Adler describes in terms of that between *substance* and *form* found within the work of Marx.[88] The forces are the real substance of social processes but they are mediated and expressed in the form of the antagonistic social relations specific to capitalist society. But rather than a simplistic unidirectional relationship, its dialectical character means that each work upon the other, such that class conflict between labour and capital is the expression of the contradiction between the forces and relations of production and vice versa. This is because the development of the forces implies the greater potential for cooperation and 'political action' on the part of the working class, through the more sophisticated and interdependent divisions of labour it affords and the expansion of knowledge and, thus, power that it grants workers. Adler, as part of this, proposes that work organisation and skills can be included in a broadened conception of the forces of production. In this respect, Adler pleads guilty to the charge of technological determinism only insofar as such an approach 'conceptually orders the relative roles' of different forces, and does not grant or deny any an absolute 'causal weight'.[89]

This understanding of substance and form implies that paleo-Marxism views the labour process through the prism of the overall valorisation process through which capital pursues profit and society attains its surplus. Connecting paleo-Marxism with a broader heterodox Marxian inheritance, Adler credits the Frankfurt School thinker Alfred Sohn-Rethel with associating scientific management, specifically in its Taylorist guise, with the objective and subjective 'socialisation' of production, both internally among the workforce and externally vis-à-vis the market.[90] Following Sohn-Rethel, Adler sees the valorisation process as a 'form' imposed upon the 'content' of the labour process.[91] Changes in the specific content of labour do not debilitate the conditions through which the valorisation process imposes its calculative logic upon production. For paleo-Marxism, the valorisation process, by driving competition between capitals, has the effect of driving both upgrading of working practices through greater socialisation of knowledge and collectivisation of experiences as well as processes of intensification and exploitation. Bureaucracy therefore has both an enabling and coercive effect.[92] In the former, socialisation has the 'socially synthetic' character Sohn-Rethel saw market exchange achieving, centring on the greater social and collective character workers and their knowledge attain. But this formal determination of the substance of labour, whilst displaying the higher-level tendency to drive progress, can also stymy it.

In light of this contradiction between substance and form, Adler suggests that Marx presents two competing and seemingly contradictory tendencies across his work.[93] The first characterised capitalist development in terms of deskilling, degradation and proletarianisation. The second characterised it in terms of upskilling, upgrading and professionalisation. Adler interprets the connection between the two resting in the different temporalities they inhabit, in Marx's work and in reality itself. The first is short-run and contingent, and essentially acts as a countertendency to the long run and determinant tendency of the second. For Adler, one of the weaknesses of LPT is that it either sees the former as the long-run tendency, stressing degradation in the relations of production rather than upgrading through the forces, or, alternatively, displays a tendency to focus on micro-level and short-run swings in the balance of control and resistance in the workplace at the expense of recognising larger-scale, longer-run tendencies around the dialectic between the forces and relations of production—specifically as they relate to technological developments.[94] For paleo-Marxism, mean-while, it is possible to see overall an upgrading tendency pegged back at various points by countertendencies owing to factors like competition and decentralised decision making.

For its part, LPT also accepts that competitive pressures and the bal-ance of class forces in the workplace and politics or society at large render upgrading and degrading tendencies contingent. But, for paleo-Marxist crit-ics, labour process approaches take a romanticised and conservative view that overstates the prevalence and sustainability of skilled or craft jobs in early capitalism.[95] Working from a critique of Braverman's deskilling thesis, paleo-Marxism proposes that the capitalist labour process is characterised by technological advancement that affords workers socialized knowledge by means of the 'mobilisation of science'.[96] The pressures of valorisation, paleo-Marxism suggests, compel firms to engage in 'a process of social-ization in which workers' skills are upgraded and the individual worker is replaced by an interdependent "collective worker"'.[97] In this sense, the elimination of craft or skilled elements of labour with new responsibilities to operate or tend machines does not, contrary to LPT, represent a loss of power or control for workers.[98] Rather, in the stripping away of labour's specificity, workers develop new forms of power and control in superintend-ing machines and the responsibility and leverage that follows—objectifying in an external reality their subjectivity with potentially emancipatory impli-cations. As Adler writes,

> Deskilling bears the same relation to separation as, in a more philo-sophical domain, alienation bears to objectification: in both pairs, both terms refer to real processes . . . [there is] thus . . . an important sense in which Marx saw the destruction of craft skills as having an emancipa-tory significance.[99]

LPT, meanwhile, has tended to take a sanguine view of how the bringing together of workers in large workplace settings in the late nineteenth century gave rise to a historically unprecedented '*objective socialisation of labour*'. This process served to definitively replace the forms of subjective sociali-sation that characterised earlier, more autonomous, kinds of cooperation such as the collective work of agricultural communities pre-capitalism. As a result of the greater sophistication and complexity in the division of labour, 'the "modern" factory allowed employers to develop much more effective and sophisticated methods of increasing the intensity of labour, rather than its mere duration'.[100] For LPT, this framework of managerial and techno-logical control to some extent 'locks in' the subordination of workers, and its path trajectory cannot simply be appropriated or transformed by workers for anti- or post-capitalist purposes. But, sensing a progressive potential for socialisation in the labour process, paleo-Marxism sees 'enabling' consequences in the 'mediated character through which socialisation proceeds in capitalist society'. This socialisation of labour occurs both directly in production itself by means of the conscious management of production by workers and indirectly through its 'mediation by market exchange', both in the buying and selling of labour power and in the exchange of the goods and services they produce by means of money.[101] Adler suggests that firms develop a whole panoply of management techniques to master what Marx calls the 'cooperation' necessary to coordinate this interdependent 'series of social acts' undertaken by the collective worker.[102] In this way, the valorisation process stimulates socialisation but in an alienated fashion, a situation against which the unfolding forces of production progressively push. Managers and workers alike act in service of the liberating development of the forces of production, stymied only by the anachronistic relations of production—in other words, the pursuit of profit that characterises the valorisation process.

Direct socialisation, on this account, remains an eventual aim of worker's struggle, something outlined in greater programmatic detail in Adler's recent book, *The 99% Economy*.[103] The revolutionary potential Adler sees concealed in this state of affairs rests in how the process

> creat[es] a working class that is increasingly educated, cognitively sophisticated, experienced in large-scale collaborative enterprise—and thus increasingly capable of taking on the task of radically transforming society and of assuming the leading role in a new form of society.[104]

Where 'core' LPT grants class struggle a contingent role in capitalist social relations, paleo-Marxism returns instead to something akin to the 'gravedigger thesis' which is said to colour some strands of traditional Marxism.[105] Class subjectivity determined at the material and economic base, the 'advancing forces of production' set 'the direction of class struggle'.[106] Hence, the capacity for class struggle is therefore determined by the technological evolution of the forces of production, the development and socialisation of which is said to lead humanity towards socialism. This latter state centres on the rational planning of production under a new set of property and political relations fit for a new society hatched 'in the womb' of the old.[107]

By this account, the problem is that capitalism 'retards' this positive evolution as relations of production compel firms to 'valorise invested capital' in 'search for profit'. But this does not mean that management practices cannot play their part in fostering progress. In particular, paleo-Marxism suggests that managerial strategies of work organisation—such as 'the principles of bureaucracy, Taylorism, or lean production'—are themselves 'part of the forces of production'. Because the forces of production represent the possibility of favourable social transformation, this opens the possibility that managers and their strategies occupy a place on the side of the arc of progress. Indeed, the planning that takes place in the context of a large, vertically integrated firm is seen by Adler as prefiguring the planning that would bring into existence a completely new type of society. The socialisation of labour that takes place within the forces of production by virtue of new managerial techniques comes to represent 'a step towards more rational, conscious planning and management of large-scale, interdependent operations'. This means that big corporates have something to offer the creation of radical alternatives, 'reminding us of Marx's dictum that history often progresses by its bad side'. But there are constraints placed upon the capacity of these corporates to properly inaugurate a new kind of society by the classed social relations that, in the paleo-Marxist account, spring from these very same forces of production.[108] Their radical potential to incubate a new society in the shell of the old is ultimately limited by the intractable contradiction presented by its purpose to pump money up to shareholders, to the benefit of one class above others.

Paleo-Marxism's theorisation of the relationship between the context of capitalist valorisation, management decision-making and the socialisation and upskilling of the collective labouring subject has inspired empirical case studies on topics including the subjective socialisation of workers in manufacturing, organisational learning as a crucible for socialisation, and the relationship between collective agency and the development of productive relations.[109] A specific focus in this research has been on Taylorist scientific management and bureaucracy as forums for the socialisation of labour and knowledge in capitalist work organisation—seen as reaching their apex in contemporary forms of production indebted to Toyotism. A particular site of empirical study where these analyses have been developed to impressive effect is high-tech, high-skill manufacturing settings, including, most notably, Adler's research at New United Motor Manufacturing, Inc (NUMMI), a joint venture between GM and Toyota.[110]

Taylorist scientific management measured individual worker performance with time-and-motion studies, producing collective standards of the 'one best way' to accomplish tasks.[111] This system had the advantage of 'removing managerial bias in capturing field data' and establishing clear and commonly understood metrics workers negotiated over through trade unions.[112] What this strand of research thus shows is that bureaucracy and scientific management mark not only simply an 'offensive in the class struggle' but also a 'progressive step in the socialisation of the forces of production, both objective and subjective'. Scientific management achieves efficiency through planning 'informed by a body of socialised knowledge' rather than 'isolated, local struggles between workers and their bosses'. Taylorism formalised private knowledge as social in bureaucratic processes of rationalisation and standardisation.[113] The social character of the knowledge driving it removed the 'mystery' from the process, even while rendering its management more impersonal.

Meanwhile, the greater complexity of the division of labour instituted under Taylorism generates a 'collective worker' comprising manifold perspectives and functions. Bureaucratic scientific management still proceeds in these empirical contexts 'under capitalist authority', repetitiveness eroding autonomy and traditional resistance. But at the same time, it grants workers wage, skill and productivity gains, reduces 'arbitrary personal authority', and extends worker organisation and solidarity across professions.[114] Increasingly managers step to one side of production and superintend the autonomous collaboration of workers on the shopfloor, rather than police it intensely as did the clipboard-wielding Taylorist manager. But this is not a seamless or uncomplicated process. The 'indirect socialisation' the valorisation process imposes upon the labour process under scientific management creates a tendency towards exploitation whilst simultaneously constructing bonds between workers in resistance against that exploitation. Together, these tendencies produce a situation whereby, stimulated by 'valorisation pressures', the formalisation and standardisation of workplace life grants knowledge an increasingly social character and the labour process an increasingly collective quality whilst also establishing processes and structures through which working practices and the 'organizational architecture' that supports them can be understood and challenged by workers. Workers do this through channels of 'conflict resolution' and 'bureaucratic escalation' that depersonalise and formalise class struggle in the workplace. At the same time, 'bureaucratic formalization and standardization of routines' can also act as 'weapons of coercion', underpinned by 'the conflictuality of the employment relation'.[115] All in all, this is not so different to some of the analyses offered by 'core' LPT. The key difference is the view of the overall, longer-run tendency for technological development to act as a positive force accomplishing upskilling and upgrading.

In Adler's long-running case study research, NUMMI shows that the legacy of this mode of scientific management had seen its most productive and positive elements taken forward in the context of 'lean production'. Lean production implied greater discretion among small, flexibly specialised teams over the setting of standards and targets, devolving autonomy and responsibility to workers so as to extract greater effort through a more consensual management style that, for Adler, pointed towards a 'high road' into the future. Whereas for LPT, the critique of deskilling is informed by the understanding in the 'younger Marx' of work as 'self-realization', for Adler and other paleo-Marxists, the coexistence of high skills and 'job boredom' in technologically augmented labour points towards the 'antiwork utopia' projected in the 'later' Marx's discussions of free time. By advocating the first of these, Adler claims, LPT requires a wholesale 'replacement' of capitalism that, owing to its impossibility, is implied to produce a pessimistic and quiescent politics. Adler argues that LPT cannot conceive of a contradiction between two real forces—the forces and relations of production—only between the paralysing distinction of 'what is' and 'what ought to be'.[116] As such, paleo-Marxism holds stocks in the favourable 'evolution' of a new society *within* capitalism, and, eventually, beyond it.

In putting 'history on the side of radical change' in such a way, paleo-Marxism has been criticised for its positive, depoliticised rendering of managerial techniques and technological innovations.[117] Its optimistic appraisal, it has been claimed, fails to capture the complex dialectical character of the relationship between the forces and relations of production. Antagonistic social relations specific to capitalist society both constitute and constrain the development of the productive forces with unpredictable rather than inevitable consequences. Walter Benjamin observed how a teleological reading of Marx led socialists of the 1920s and the 1930s to wrongly believe that it was sufficient to simply 'move with the current' and let the forces of production deliver labour the world it was theirs to inherit.[118] But, as Adorno noted, the dialectic need not always move forward, but rather grows in on itself, contradictions and dysfunctions intensifying without closure or favourable resolution.[119] Social forms express and temporarily fix in place these social relations at the level of the valorisation process or the circuit of capital as a whole: value, money and, namely, the state as itself a form of capitalist social relations. The state, in particular, plays a vital role in maintaining what Adorno calls the 'static side' of the dialectic, at the expense of a dialectical 'dynamic'. This much can be seen in the fact—noted by scholars loosely associated with paleo-Marxist critiques like Matt Vidal—that tendencies towards more productive management practices and enriched, engaged job environments are in scant evidence today, with a pervasive productivity puzzle and precarious, low-skilled service economy providing few of the fruits some analyses promise, a state of affairs fixed in place by the prevailing policy context.[120]

The issue of productivity and the lagging profitability and dynamism of Western economies over the long downturn beginning in the 1970s throws into sharp relief the differences between 'core' LPT and its paleo-Marxist internal critique. Paleo-Marxists like Adler see both classes—workers and capitalists—having an interest in rising productivity. Conflict and resistance can contribute to productivity rather than debilitate it, with trades unions and collective bargaining expanding worker voice and ensuring that productivity gains are shared in mutually rather than fought over in a zero-sum game.[121] Additionally, Adler and Borys cite evidence that automation and skill are closely correlated, insofar as mechanisation creates new skilled jobs, enhances job content in existing roles and changes the overall composition of the labour market towards new product lines, skills and professions.[122] But, according to Thompson, Adler conceives of productivity and skill trends as if Fordist-Keynesianism is still the structuring principle of capitalist political economy.[123] This fails to account for the decline of profitability and productivity in Western capitalist production from the 1970s onwards, which in turn saw capital flock to financialised channels of revenue-raising, in turn reshaping the contemporary workplace, the rule of shareholder value subsequently disincentivising the investment in new technologies and techniques that would enable any industrial revival. Pending a resurrection of a social-industrial compromise such as that which underpinned the Fordist-Keynesian era—perhaps via the coming new 'cold war' some foresee—the opportunities for the forces of production to unfold as paleo-Marxists propose seem sorely lacking.

Conclusion

By revitalising the study of the labour process through the prism of the valorisation process, 'core' LPT maintains a consistent, if sometimes implicit or critical, connection with key themes of Marx's CoPE. Inspired by the perspectives this generates, labour process scholars continue to offer cutting-edge confrontations with contemporary currents of mainstream and radical thought about the changing world of work.[124] In particular, they represent a vital counterweight to hype about the future of work. Perspectives on the labour process show that instead of productive investment in skills, new techniques and management practices befitting of the futures of work we are informed lie imminently in wait, financialised capitalism has sweated service-based human-centred labour in pursuit of shareholder value, using a range of cost-cutting and coercive techniques that make technological wizardry an expensive waste of money. This is underpinned by an absence of effective channels for autonomous worker power that in previous times has helped motivate employers to technologically revolutionise the labour process and enabled workers to share gains from productivity improvements and the generation of a surplus. Without a framework for achieving and sharing gains from production, workers have little way to compel improvements and lay claim to the full value of their work.

In this sense, its perspective on the labour process in its full social, political and economic context makes LPT particularly averse to popular claims of change or even elimination of work. Micro-level changes in the labour process do not necessarily imply wider transformations in capitalist society, because the character of the valorisation process and the 'circuit of capital as a whole' persist independent of specific material shifts in production— namely, the foundational pursuit of profit, and search for surplus, on which the reproduction of capitalist society hinges. Moreover, LPT provides no easy answers for a positive resolution to the politics of production, stressing contingency between the workplace and any project of wider social transformation, the interconnections between the two mediated by indeterminate cultural and social factors rather than subject to any direct or inevitable relationship between the economic 'base' and political 'superstructure'.

This approach to the labour process, contrary to the critiques it receives, remains generously open to combination within other frames. Setting out only to pursue the limited and specific aim of comprehending the labour process as a site where wider social relations are mediated, LPT makes no claim to a totalising theory and thus can be augmented and complemented by other approaches that capture other moments of the social totality in order to grasp how the labour process is shaped by forms and relations that lie beyond it. In this way, as we shall see, other theories offer fresh perspectives that help refocus the zoom lens LPT offers on the labour process.

Notes

1 Braverman H (1974) *Labour and Monopoly Capital*. New York: Vintage; Burawoy M (1979) *Manufacturing Consent*. London: Verso; Burawoy M (1985) *Politics of Production*. London: Verso; Edwards R (1979) *Contested Terrain*. New York: Basic Books; Edwards P (1986) *Conflict at Work*. Oxford: Blackwell; Friedman A (1977) *Industry and Labour*. London: Macmillan; Smith C (2015) Rediscovery of the labour process. In: Edgell S, Gottfried H, Granter E (eds.) *The Sage Handbook of the Sociology of Work and Employment*, Los Angeles: SAGE, pp. 205–224; Thompson P (1989) *The Nature of Work*. London: Macmillan.
2 Smith 2015: 206.
3 Burawoy M (1983) Between the labor process and the state. *American Sociological Review* 48(5): 587–605.
4 Braverman 1974.
5 Smith 2015: 212.
6 Carter B (2020) Defending Marx and Braverman: Taking back the labour process in theory and practice. *International Socialism*. Available at: https://isj.org.uk/marx-and-braverman/
7 Smith 2015: 210; Thompson 1989: 4.
8 Smith C (2006) The double indeterminacy of labour power. *Work, Employment and Society* 20(2): 389–402.

9 Thompson 1989: 242.
10 Thompson P (1990) Crawling from the wreckage. In: Knights D, Willmott H (eds.) *Labour Process Theory*. London: MacMillan, p. 100; Thompson P, Smith C (2001) Follow the Red Brick Road. *International Studies of Management and Organization* 30: 40–67 (56–57).
11 Burawoy 1979: 16; Thompson 1989: 154.
12 Thompson 1989: 48.
13 Taylor G (2002) Labour and subjectivity. In: Dinerstein A, Neary M (eds.) *The Labour Debate*. Aldershot: Ashgate, pp. 89–107 (93).
14 Rowlinson M, Hassard J (1994) Economics, politics and labour process theory. *Capital & Class* 18: 65–97; Lucio MM, Stewart P (1997) The paradox of contemporary labour process theory. *Capital & Class* 21(2): 49–77; Spencer DA (2000) Braverman and the contribution of labour process analysis to the critique of capitalist production—twenty-five years on. *Work, Employment and Society* 14(2): 223–243.
15 Thompson 1989: 242–249.
16 Thompson 1989: 250.
17 Knights D, Willmott H (1990) *Labour Process Theory*. London: Macmillan.
18 Parker M (1999) Capitalism, subjectivity and ethics. *Organization Studies* 20(1): 25–45.
19 Thompson P (2010) The capitalist labour process. *Capital & Class* 34(1): 7–14 (9).
20 Cressey P, MacInnes J (1980) Voting for Ford. *Capital & Class* 11: 2–37 (5).
21 Gandini A (2019) Labour process theory and the gig economy. *Human Relations* 72(6): 1039–1056 (1044); Thompson 1990: 102.
22 Thompson P, Vincent S (2010) Labour process theory and critical realism. In: *Working Life*. London: Palgrave, pp. 47–69; Jaros SJ (2005) Marxian critiques of Thompson's 'core' labour process theory. *Ephemera* 5(1): 5–25.
23 Thompson 1990: 115.
24 Burawoy 1985: 5–6, 112.
25 Thompson 1989: 246.
26 Brighton Labour Process Group (1977) The capitalist labour process. *Capital & Class* 1: 3–24 (23–24).
27 Cressey & MacInnes 1980: 20–29.
28 Carter B (1995) A growing divide. *Capital & Class* 19(1): 33–72; Lucio & Stewart 1997; Rowlinson & Hassard 1994.
29 Carter 2020; Smith C, Willmott H (1991) The new middle class and the labour process. In: *White-Collar Work*. London: Palgrave, pp. 13–34.
30 Edwards P (1990) Understanding conflict in the labour process. In: Knights D, Willmott H (eds.) *Labour Process Theory*. London: Macmillan, pp. 125–152.
31 Thompson 1989: 4, 231–233, 243.
32 Jaros 2005; Cohen S (1987) A labour process to nowhere? *New Left Review* 165: 34–50; Kelly J (1985) Management's redesign of work. In: Knights D, Willmott H, Collinson DL (eds.) *Job Redesign*. London: Gower, pp. 30–51.
33 Reveley J (2011) Management's critical turn. *Science and Society* 75(3): 325–347 (328–329).
34 Edwards 1990.
35 Jaros 2005; Reveley 2011: 329.
36 Cohen 1987; Kelly 1985.
37 Thompson 1990: 100.

38 Jaros 2005; Cohen 1987: 48; Spencer 2000.
39 Thompson 1989: 4, 231–233.
40 Thompson 1989: 41, 233–234; Smith 2015: 214.
41 Smith 2015: 214; Burawoy 1983: 587.
42 Newsome K (2015) Value in motion. In: *Putting Labour in Its Place*. London: Palgrave, 29–45.
43 Taylor P, Newsome K, Rainnie A (2013) Putting labour in its place. *Competition & Change* 17(1): 1–5; Hauptmeier M, Vidal M (eds.) (2014) *Comparative Political Economy of Work*. London: Palgrave.
44 Parker R, Cox S, Thompson P (2018) Financialization and value-based control. *Economic Geography* 94(1): 49–67; Cushen J, Thompson P (2020) Value logics and labor: Collateral damage or central focus? In: *The Routledge International Handbook of Financialization*. Abingdon: Routledge, pp. 324–329.
45 Burawoy 1983; Ngai P, Smith C (2007) Putting transnational labour process in its place. *Work, Employment & Society* 21(1): 27–45; Smith C, Liu M (2016) In search of the labour process perspective in China. In: *China at Work*. London: Palgrave Macmillan, pp. 1–30; Hauptmeier & Vidal 2014; Thompson & Vincent 2010.
46 Smith 2015: 207; Thompson 1989: 41.
47 Smith 2015: 212.
48 Edwards 1979.
49 Edwards 1986.
50 Burawoy 1985.
51 Cressey & MacInnes 1980.
52 Thompson 1989: 59.
53 Friedman 1977.
54 Thompson 1989: 133.
55 Thompson 1989: 136–137.
56 Thompson 1989: 133.
57 Cressey & MacInnes 1980.
58 Burawoy 1979; Thompson 1989: 52.
59 See a full list of contributions to the International Labour Process Conference book series here: www.ilpc.org.uk/Book-Series.
60 Böhm S, Land C (2012) The new 'hidden abode'. *Sociological Review* 60(2): 217–240.
61 Beverungen A, Böhm S, Land C (2015) Free labour, social media, management. *Organization Studies* 36(4): 473–489.
62 Thompson P (2005) Foundation and empire. *Capital & Class* 86: 73–100.
63 McKinlay A, Smith C (eds.) (2009) *Creative Labour*. London: Palgrave, 15.
64 Thompson P, Jones M, Warhurst C (2007) From conception to consumption. *Journal of Organizational Behaviour* 28: 625–640.
65 Thompson P, Parker R, Cox S (2016) Interrogating creative theory and creative work. *Sociology* 50(2): 316–332 (328).
66 Thompson et al. 2007: 626.
67 Reveley 2011: 329.
68 Thompson & Vincent 2010; Thompson P, Smith C (2009) Labour power and labour process. *Sociology* 43(5): 913–930 (923).
69 Thompson P (2013) Financialization and the workplace. *Work, Employment and Society* 27(3): 472–488; Cushen J, Thompson P (2016) Financialization

and value. *Work, Employment and Society* 30(2): 352–365; Parker et al. 2018; Cushen & Thompson 2020.

70   Cushen & Thompson 2020: 324.
71   Thompson 2003.
72   Thompson 2013: 483.
73   Cushen & Thompson 2016: 353–362.
74   Cushen & Thompson 2016: 358–360.
75   Parker et al. 2018: 53.
76   Parker et al. 2018: 64.
77   Cushen & Thompson 2020: 326.
78   Cushen & Thompson 2020: 326–327.
79   Burawoy 1983: 588; Thompson 1989: 243.
80   Adler PS (2004) Skill trends under capitalism and the socialisation of production. In: Warhurst C, Grugulis I, Keep W (eds.) *The Skills That Matter*. Houndmills: Palgrave Macmillan, pp. 242–260; Thompson P (2020) Capitalism, Technology and Work. *Political Quarterly* 91(2): 299–309; Findlay P, Thompson P (2017) Contemporary work. *Journal of Industrial Relations* 59(2): 122–138.
81   Thompson 1989: 4.
82   Thompson 2020.
83   Reveley 2011: 325; Adler P (2007) The future of critical management studies. *Organization Studies* 28(9): 1313–1345; Adler P (2009) Marx and organization studies today. In: *Oxford Handbook of Sociology and Organization Studies*. Oxford: Oxford University Press, pp. 62–91; Adler P (2012) The sociological ambivalence of bureaucracy. *Organization Science* 23(1): 244–266.
84   Adler 2007: 1313.
85   Reveley 2011; Ingvaldsen JA (2015) Organizational learning. *Organization Studies* 36(4): 423–444.
86   Delbridge R (2007) Explaining conflicted collaboration. *Organization Studies* 28: 1347–1357 (1347).
87   Reveley 2011.
88   Adler P (1990) Marx, machines, and skill. *Technology and Culture* 31(4): 780–812 (784).
89   Adler 1990: 788–789.
90   Adler 2004: 8; Sohn-Rethel A (1978) *Intellectual and Manual Labour*. London: Macmillian.
91   Adler 2012.
92   Adler P, Borys B (1996) Two types of bureaucracy: Enabling and coercive. *Administrative Science Quarterly* 41(1): 61–89.
93   Adler 1990.
94   Adler P, Borys B (1989) Automation and skill. *Politics & Society* 17(3): 377–402 (378).
95   Adler & Borys 1989.
96   Adler 2007: 1321; Ingvaldsen 2015: 428.
97   Ingvaldsen 2015: 428.
98   Adler & Borys 1989.
99   Adler 1990: 783.
100   Thompson 1989: 43–51.
101   Adler 2012: 251.
102   Adler 2007: 1321; Marx 1976: Ch. 13.

103 Adler P (2019) *The 99 Percent Economy*. Oxford: Oxford University Press.
104 Ingvaldsen 2015: 428; Adler 2007: 1328.
105 Vidal M (2018) Was Marx wrong about the working class? Reconsidering the gravedigger thesis. *International Socialism: A Quarterly Review of Socialist Theory* issue 158.
106 Adler 2009: 64; Delbridge 2007: 1347.
107 Ingvaldsen 2015: 435.
108 Adler 2007: 1321–1324; Adler 2009: 79; Ingvaldsen 2015.
109 Maravelias C, Thanem T, Holmqvist M (2013) March meets Marx. In: Spicer A (ed.) *Managing 'Human Resources' By Exploiting and Exploring People's Potentials*. Bingley: Emerald, pp. 129–159; Ingvaldsen 2015; Maielli G (2015) Explaining organizational paths through the concept of Hegemony. *Organizational Studies* 34(4): 491–511.
110 Adler P (1999) Teams at NUMMI. In: *Teamwork in the Automobile Industry*. London: Palgrave, pp. 126–150. Adler P, Goldoftas B, Levine DI (1997) Ergonomics, employee involvement, and the Toyota Production System. *ILR Review* 50(3): 416–437.
111 The paragraphs that follow draw from Pitts FH (2020a) Measuring and managing creative labour. *Organization*. doi:10.1177/1350508420968187
112 Gregg M (2016) The athleticism of accomplishment. In: Wajcman J, Dodd N (eds.) *The Sociology of Speed*. Oxford: Oxford University Press, pp. 102–116 (105–106).
113 Adler 2012: 252–254.
114 Adler 2004: 8–9.
115 Adler 2012: 252–254.
116 Adler 1990: 783–786.
117 Thompson P (2007) Adler's theory of the capitalist labour process. *Organization Studies* 28(9): 1359–1368; Vallas S (2007) Paleo-paralysis? *Organization Studies* 28(9): 1379–1385.
118 Benjamin W (1999) Theses on the philosophy of history. In: *Illuminations*. London: Pimlico, 245–255 (249–250).
119 Adorno TW (1990) *Negative Dialectics*. London: Routledge; Adorno TW (2003a) Reflections on class theory. In: Tiedemann R (ed.) *Can One Live After Auschwitz?* Stanford: Stanford University Press, pp. 93–110.
120 Vidal M (2019) Contradictions of the labour process, worker empowerment and capitalist inefficiency. *Historical Materialism* 28(2): 170–204. As the manuscript was being finalised Vidal announced a new book bringing together his innovative empirical and theoretical work on this topic: Vidal M (forthcoming) *Management Divided*. Oxford: Oxford University Press.
121 Adler & Borys 1989.
122 Adler & Borys 1989.
123 Thompson 2007.
124 See, for instance, the first edition of a new journal whose first edition was published at the time work was being completed on this chapter: *Work in the Global Economy* (Bristol University Press).

3 Beyond the hidden abode
From class composition to the crisis of value

Introduction

In the previous chapter, we entered the hidden abode of production, encountering Labour Process Theory (LPT), which, whilst keeping a keen eye on the valorisation process, maintains a primary focus on managerial control in the organisation of work itself. In this chapter, we chart theories that attempt to go *beyond* the hidden abode of production, examining the processes of class struggle and social transformation that take place not only within the traditional workplace but also without it. We will do so through a discussion of *autonomist* strands of Marxism. Autonomist Marxism, in its various guises, is an approach to the study of work and organisation that has influenced a string of studies in management and organisation studies (MOS) over recent years.[1] In its dominant form, it originates in the 1960s and the 1970s with the work of Italian *workerists*. Central here is a 'Copernican Inversion' foregrounding the power of workers to propel history towards the overcoming of capitalism through class struggle, as opposed to the hitherto dominant orthodox Marxist understanding of the working class as a 'passive, reactive victim, which defends its interest against capitalist onslaught'.[2] This conceptualisation grants workers the power of self-valorisation, which places capital in the position of having to control, constrain and capture the value produced by them.

Workerism owes its roots to Italian scholars and activists such as Mario Tronti, Roman Alquati, Raniero Panzieri and Sergio Bologna.[3] It was popularised outside the Italian context on the Anglophone left by groups such as the Conference of Socialist Economists, Big Flame and the Zerowork Collective.[4] As a distinct strand of autonomist Marxism, workerists were interested in 'the laws of development' through which 'the economic input labour power periodically constituted itself as the political subject working class'.[5] 'Class composition', in this sense, is the 'forms of behaviour' that result from the 'ongoing interplay between the articulations of labour power

DOI: 10.4324/9781003198895-3

produced by capitalist development, and labour's struggles to overcome them'.[6] This movement centres on processes of 'decomposition' through which capital fragments the working class, and processes of 'recomposition' through which the working class arranges itself in response. Which of these processes—decomposition or recomposition—had primacy at any one point was a crucial bone of political contention within Italian workerism.[7]

Later, *post-workerism* came to supplant workerism in the radical imaginary, expressing a broader shift within the left away from a politics of work and class, locating power and resistance beyond the workplace in society at large within the diffuse non-class of the 'multitude'. Post-workerism differentiated itself from the early workerism of its adherents by seeing liberation arising not from an antagonistic relationship with labour but through that labour itself. By seeing labour under capitalism sowing the seeds of its own liberation, every development in capitalism was met with an unremitting positivity. Particularly of note in the contemporary reception of these ideas in modern MOS scholarship are Michael Hardt and Antonio Negri's now long-running series of books on the development of political power and resistance in contemporary capitalism, which have had a relationship of influence and reflection with radical left politics over the past 20 years. *Empire* and *Multitude* combined eulogies to the transformative potential of the New Economy with a theorisation of the alterglobalisation struggles ensuing at the turn of the millennium.[8] *Commonwealth* and *Declaration*, meanwhile, traced the emergence of the post-crisis social movements that took the horizontalist politics of those earlier struggles into public spaces and popular imaginaries.[9] In *Assembly*, the latest instalment in Hardt and Negri's continuing engagement with capitalism and its alternatives in the contemporary time, the authors harden the technologically determinist and post-humanist tenor of their work by interweaving this imaginary with an electoralist 'institutional turn' towards the state that leads them to distance themselves from the horizontalist politics both absorbed in and informed by their previous works.[10]

Workerism, meanwhile, remained more circumspect about the organisational shifts post-workerism eulogised, even whilst analysing the same kinds of creative or entrepreneurial labour that post-workerist analyses came to fixate upon.[11] Out of the shadow post-workerism cast, today we see a renewed interest in its workerist precursor and the central role it granted labour in processes of class composition and the formation of political subjectivity. As we will see, it finds particular relevance applied to the modes of resistance and activism produced by the technological and organisational innovations of the digital economy. The reception of such autonomist approaches in MOS has been mediated by the 'political contention' that cascaded from the financial crisis, which 'catalysed the development of a generation of Marxist intellectuals who acted as the *avant garde*' of a so-called 'generation left' searching 'for new theoretical and methodological tools with which to understand the re-emergence of overt class struggle'.[12] This chapter charts how the uptake of these ideas in MOS is increasingly split between post-workerist-influenced analyses and autonomist Marxist approaches more in keeping with the insights of original workerist thinkers.

Class composition from workerism to post-workerism

We begin with the concept of class composition, which acted as a conceptual skeleton key for the workerist left in Italy in the 1960s and 1970s.[13] Workerism stressed the relationship between the *technical* composition, or 'material structure', of the working class and its *political* composition—'its behaviour as a subject autonomous from the dictates of both the labour movement and capital'.[14] The former represents 'the organization of the working class by capital', and incorporates conditions like how labour is divided, managed and mechanised, as well as, in some accounts, 'the "forms of reproduction", such as community and family structures, through which the class relation is perpetuated'. The political composition, meanwhile, represents 'the organizational capacity of the working class to fight for its own needs and development', incorporating modes of 'refusal, resistance and re-appropriation of surplus value'.[15]

Workerism applied this framework to analyse 'working-class behaviour in the most advanced sectors of the economy' at any one time, as a window into the 'political laws of motion' of labour and capitalist development.[16] Workerism originally refused the temporally and spatially rigid relationship between the material and the subjective posited by orthodox Marxism, assigning no inevitability to the progression from the technical to the political composition.[17] The conviction that classes were composed through struggle overcame the orthodox Marxist understanding of the working class as sharing only an original state of dispossession, the incoherence of which led Leninists to propose a party or vanguard to bring order and discipline to its disparate parts.[18] Refusing to force all workers into the straightjacket of a premature unanimity based on the experience of exploitation, workerism recognised that forms of organisation like unions and parties expressed 'the concrete character of the class relation' only in certain historically specific circumstances appropriate to the requirements of its recomposition.[19] Hence, whilst the relationship between the workplace and political subjectivity undoubtedly possessed an underlying directionality for early workerists, the most sophisticated among them saw the form it assumed as contingent.

Thus, for foundational workerists like Panzieri, class recomposition was not simply a result of the organic composition between variable and constant capital at a given stage of capitalist development, but itself a catalyst for the latter's reorganisation. In this way, the shifting organic composition is 'not the outcome of a neutral, purely scientific process of technological progress', but rather the result of capital's political and economic drive to 'decompose' the working class. But each successive attempt at decomposition also provides the basis for recomposition, through a new technical composition that, for instance, permitted workers under Taylorism the power to 'stop the line', and generated the institutional power wielded by the 'mass worker' under Fordism.[20] The mass worker was the sum of 'individual labour powers' politically composed through struggles, the militancy of which provoked capital to technologically revolutionise the labour process at pivotal sites of workerist activism and analysis like FIAT Turin.[21]

Whilst this 'Copernican inversion' of class perspective escaped the 'economic rationality' of orthodox Marxism, workerism still tended to presume the presence of an intrinsically antagonistic class subject whose 'material articulation' within the technical composition at the point of production would generate a political composition focused on the revolutionary overthrow of its subordination 'in pursuit of a new political unity'. However, this determinism elided the 'contradictory reality' of working-class life and the varying forms of political behaviour through which it is expressed.[22] Moreover, the primacy awarded the technical composition in explaining political behaviour increasingly ran counter to workerism's founding assumption that workers played an autonomous role in driving capitalist development.[23]

One response to this impasse was to deny 'any necessary relationship between the labour process and class behaviour', as did groups like *Potere Operaiao*, although this theoretical manoeuvre could be carried off only by displacing the moment of determination of revolutionary subjectivity from the point of production to society at large. For *Potere Operaiao*, the material articulation between the technical and the political composition assumed a 'much larger and more pregnant' form with the expansion of the capital relation beyond the factory'.[24] This meant dismissing, as did Alquati, any 'simple, clearcut distinction . . . between the plants where surplus value is created, the residential zones where labour power reproduces itself, and the centres of administration'.[25] Chiming with the 'factory-city' organised around FIAT workers and their families in Turin, Tronti's concept of the 'social factory' highlighted the role of the 'home and the community', as well as 'schools and welfare offices', in the reproduction, education and socialisation of the working class. The political implication was that action in this domain could thus strike at the heart of the production of labour power itself, and groups like *Lotta Continua* moved from the factory to the city streets, fighting for the 'self-reduction of housing, food and utility prices'.[26]

For these analyses, the social and industrial compromise constructed around the mass worker was exploded not only by working-class refusal of the wage-productivity bargain but also by the students, women, anti-war and Black power movements.[27] These shifts, some workerists thought, represented the 'annihilation' of 'a whole culture of industrial class struggle', including both its technical composition in the labour process and its political composition in parties and unions. This raised the spectre of the decomposition of the 'very concept of class itself'.[28] This opened the workerist analysis of class composition to gender, race and culture, if only tentatively and incompletely.[29] For the emergent *post-workerist*s, meanwhile, the new social movements that surged in the space vacated by the traditional working class recomposed themselves in the form of what Alquati termed the 'social(ised) worker'.

What was initially theorised as the 'socialised worker' for the post-workerists became the 'multitude'—inspiring a level of popularity and influence across the social sciences, including MOS, far in advance of that achieved by anything workerism produced hitherto. For Negri, the mass worker represented the first clear 'concretisation' of the relationship between the progressive abstraction of labour and its socialisation. But, as a vanguard comprising only specific 'determinate sectors of the class', the concept of the 'mass worker', confined to the relationship with production, had exhausted its use. The 'social(ised) worker', meanwhile, represented a class recomposition in the face of technological change the conditions of which spanned the entire 'arc of the valorisation process' itself. The extent and universality of this new 'unity of abstract social labour' overrode 'the "specific" problems of the various sectors of the social sphere (young people, women, marginalised elements, etc.) and the factory'. From the perspective of productive relations, meanwhile, the likes of Alquati and Bifo saw the emergence of this socialised worker in the 'proletarianisation and massification' of 'intellectual and technical labour'. From the 1970s onwards, university students and intellectual workers were seen as central to this new composition, representing the 'productive intelligence' of what Marx called the 'general intellect' forged in the refusal of assembly-line working life. In particular, the law of value was seen as increasingly inadequate for the 'mediation of [the] needs and reproduction of this class of workers'.[30] As we shall see, these tendencies were later theorised through post-workerist concepts of 'immaterial labour' and the 'crisis of measurability'.

Stressing the proletarianisation and factoryisation of intellectual labour over world-shattering 'general intellect', workerist holdouts like Bologna and Alquati saw the shift from the mass worker to the socialised worker owing more to Negri's ideological abandonment of the politics of production than any substantial material change in the technical composition. Ignoring the continuities and commonalities that characterised the material conditions of work in both manual and intellectual labour, the category of the socialised worker dissolved the connection between concrete particularity and political behaviour present in the mass worker, putting in its place a mish-mash of different phenomena and antagonisms in which 'specific and contradictory' elements were ironed out. The mutation of the mass worker into, first, the socialised worker and, subsequently, the multitude vaguely described something resembling a 'generic proletariat' but that was 'yet to appear as a mature political subject'.[31] Informed by such critiques, workerism's flame was carried in Bologna's continued focus on the workplace. In his famous essay, 'The Tribe of Moles', Bologna insisted that 'the behaviour exhibited by the new social protagonists did not stem from a material location extraneous to the world of production', but rather from the incapacity of contemporary politics to grant legitimacy to the marginalised material needs attached to the changing labour process in a rising service sector characterised by self-employment, subcontracting and casual contracts.[32] For Bologna, it was precisely this decentralisation of production reshaping class composition along lines of age, geography, gender and social background.[33]

For post-workerists like Negri, this composition represented the new forms of liberation emerging through, and not against, labour itself, as the New Economy granted workers 'greater freedom and autonomy'. But, investigating working life in the same nascent creative and digital industries that formed the focal point of post-workerist analyses of 'immaterial labour', workerists like Bologna reached much different, more circumspect, conclusions. Assuming the immanent capacity of the multitude to self-organise amidst new ways of working, post-workerists underestimated the real constraints faced by the 'second-generation autonomous workforce' in replicating the continuingly relevant conditions of 'self-protection, representation of its own interests, and coalition-building' indispensable to earlier class compositions like the mass worker. The identification of the immaterial labourer with an intrinsic state of liberation functioned as a convenient distraction from the practical difficulties of mobilising labour in a new economy whose precariousness 'eradicated' the 'conditions for coalition-building', and thus obscured the concrete potential for formally autonomous or independent workers to recompose themselves as a class using more traditional organisational and institutional repertoires familiar to workerist analysis.[34]

Post-workerist MOS: immaterial labour and the crisis of measurability

The implications of class composition analysis (CCA) most readily taken up within MOS have been those associated with Hardt and Negri's post-workerist appraisal of immaterial labour, the multitude and the crisis of measurability (or crisis of the law of value). This centres on a broad empirical assessment of the contemporary conditions of labour and production that resonates through a set of wider political and economic arguments. Post-workerism follows workerism in stressing the agency of an expansive labour subject—the multitude—in determining social change and driving capitalist development, rather than management or capital itself. The multitude's spontaneous, cooperative 'self-valorisation'—exemplified in the new forms of work found in the emergent New Economy—is taken to exceed the capacity of capital to capture and control it, driving capitalist development towards a revolutionary post-capitalist transformation.

In its latest and perhaps most sophisticated rendition in *Assembly*, Hardt and Negri identify five core theses of their post-workerist approach to the understanding of labour, value and capitalism. First, they state that contemporary capitalism is dependent on forms of 'social and natural wealth' initially shared in common but increasingly expropriated and valorised by capital. This implies that capitalism is an alien imposition on a pre-existing, prelapsarian naturalness that in some way survives intact, withstanding subsumption. Second, the dependence of capital upon the common is expressed in the changing face of labour, the hegemonic forms of which exhibit cooperation, knowledge, care, affect and creativity to a much greater degree than in previous economic settlements. This, for Hardt and Negri, draws from the common and creates new commons insofar as it works from and on the production and reproduction of human relationships. This also grants labour a degree of autonomy from 'capitalist command' insofar as it is 'animated' by life beyond the workplace and the employment relationship. In this respect, the relationship between the labour process and the valorisation process is typically presented as immediate rather than mediated. In their account of the 'immediately abstract' character of contemporary labour, exchange plays no part in rendering private labours social—they are always-already social.[35] This ontological rejection of mediation has a philosophical basis—seeing reality itself as untouched by mediation—and a historical basis in that the networked sociality and cooperation of contemporary production resist organisation and management.[36] It can no longer mediate the 'uncontained, overflowing force' of the power multitude wields, which 'wells up from the field of social conflict', exceeding all limits set by capitalists and managers.[37]

Third, technological developments like digital algorithms are decentralising the capacity to gather and store knowledge such that networked young workers create and appropriate their own forms of 'fixed capital' pivotal to the kind of capitalist production Hardt and Negri see as decisive today. Fourth, this shift from traditional industries to business models based on the extraction of value from the common, whether natural or social, is not necessarily one where the latter becomes quantitatively dominant but rather a story of the qualitative significance of certain forms of activity and industry. Fifth and final, these changes at the productive base of capitalist society cascade upwards to impact upon how power governs and how resistance is organised, granting the latter autonomy and independence by means of the 'multitude' of digital and immaterial labourers who work with and upon the common, and the former a reactive and dependent existence vis-a-vis the latter.

This understanding of labour and value has a practical and political significance insofar as it celebrates and seeks the extension and reward of the multitude's productiveness through social cooperation, access to knowledge, the commoning of resources and wealth and the combination of human and non-human forces in the digital age, underpinned by policy interventions like the basic income.[38] This relevance for praxis has driven extensive empirical uptake within MOS, specifically around Hardt and Negri's diagnosis of the revolutionary potential of particular forms of contemporary capitalist production. The kinds of labour the multitude engages in have been characterised as 'immaterial' insofar as they 'produce an immaterial good, such as a service, a cultural product, knowledge or communication', and in doing so rely upon the everyday human capacity to communicate, consume, empathise, cognise, and emote.[39] Lazzarato was the first to provide a fully articulated definition of immaterial labour, as that which is productive of 'needs, the imaginary, consumer tastes and so forth'.[40] Lazzarato's immaterial labour thesis suggests that work in postindustrial economies has become based principally around the creation and manipulation of ideas, symbols, selves, emotions and relationships, inhabiting as a result the full range of human capacities and activities of which life itself consists.

As such, for those employed in these forms of production, the boundary between work time engaged in immaterial labour and spare time away from paid employment becomes increasingly indistinct, as the activities of work take on the characteristics of those of leisure and of everyday life, and those of leisure and everyday life assume the characteristics of work. As Hardt and Negri suggest,

> [w]hen production is aimed at solving a problem . . . or creating an idea or a relationship, work time tends to expand to the entire time of life. An idea or image comes to you not only in the office but also in the shower or in your dreams.[41]

In this way, the blurring of boundaries between labour time and non-labour time is, as Virno asserts, a symptom of the increasing similarity between human activity and labour activity.[42] Lazzarato claims that such labour has integrated consumption and production to such an extent that consumption is itself productive, setting into motion an immediate 'feedback loop' governed by the new creative potential of communication put to work in the labour process.[43] In this way, times of production and reproduction having become further intertwined, immaterial labour transcends the formal confines of the working day to invest the whole of life with its value-producing processes.

Influenced by this empirical and political analysis of contemporary work as increasingly 'immaterial', or centred on the manipulation of meaning, symbols and affect, as exemplified in knowledge-based forms of creative, cognitive and communicative labour, post-workerism rethinks Marxist notions of value. Immaterial labour and the value it produces spills beyond the workplace into the so-called 'social factory'. The novel historical claim in the work of Hardt and Negri and others is that contemporary 'communicative capitalism' extends this social factory to a breaking point: the production of value is so omnipresent as to smash through the boundaries of capitalist valuation and measurement altogether. The rise of this particular kind of labour is thus taken as proof of the realisation of the prophecy of capitalist breakdown portrayed in the few pages of the 'Fragment on Machines' from Marx's notebooks for *Capital*, the *Grundrisse*, read through the lens of a Spinozian philosophy of immanence.[44] Here, the technologically aided socialisation of the 'general intellect' frees workers from labour and expands free time and the production of value to the extent that capitalist measure crumbles.[45] Whereas in the Fragment on Machines, this represents a speculative vision of a far-off future, for post-workerism, it reflects an unfolding social reality. Occurring beyond the boundaries of the traditional workplace and its working day, and spontaneously productive of its own self-valorised value, immaterial labour is taken to burst through capitalist frameworks of measure and control, rendering the law of value obsolete and with it Marxian value theory.[46] This 'crisis of measurability' heralds the end of capitalism and the realisation of an incipient communism contained within its shell.[47]

In MOS, this post-workerist appraisal of the crisis of value has informed empirical research on brands, social media, the ethical economy, consumption or 'prosumption', and culture and cultural work.[48] Key foci here are how the value created by the 'free labour' of sociality and communication is captured, managed and realised by capital, and the problems that confront capital's capacity to measure value when it is produced beyond wage labour in 'the quality of social relations' themselves.[49] In particular, focus falls on 'the forms of value-productive activity . . . that occur outside of an employment relationship'—the 'free labour' identified by theorists in the post-workerist tradition like Tiziana Terranova—and the alleged crisis of measurability that it causes.[50] Due to the radically dispersed and omnipresent nature of production in contemporary capitalist society, it is claimed that the measure of labour time that formed the backbone of the classical Marxist appreciation of human labour and production is no longer adequate. Recent theorisations have located such extra-workplace immaterial production in the way in which the internet is used in one's spare time, creating value with every click.[51] It is claimed that any quantitative measure of time spent in such activities, either inside or outside the confines of the working day, cannot capture the essence of the transformation that is taking place and is not capable of embracing the immeasurable nature of such value.[52]

This process, and the proliferation of analyses of these tendencies, gathered pace in the 1990s with the rise of the new economy, whereby, hand-in-hand with 'abundant capital', arrived 'new labor cultures' facilitated by the massive investment which flowed into the hands of young, enterprising individuals hustling in the 'frontier space opened by internet commercialization'.[53] These new cultures of work entailed the expenditure of a vast amount of free and unpaid labour in connection with the immaterial and informational kinds of production at the heart of so-called 'Dot.Com' enterprises. An ethnographic account of a typical New Economy firm specialising in ICT business services describes many common traits associated with this swelling mass of free and unpaid labour, including an informal work regime which, whilst seeming hands-off, incorporates ever-more avidly the worker's own personality and self into the production process and extends the working day under the auspices of informality and fun; a reliance upon location in one's own time of the 'solving of creative problems', the building of social networks and the learning of new skills, stripping away the boundaries between work and non-work time; the recruiting of workers' innermost communicative, emotional and cognitive capacities in the servicing of the labour task, and the intertwining of the worker's fortunes with the financial outlook of the company through the award of stock options as a compartment of employee compensation. Rather than propelling a reduction in working hours, new technology such as the Internet and the constant access to information networks it facilitated had 'obliterated' the 'concept of a finite workday', such that it was not uncommon to witness 80-hour workweeks in New Economy businesses.[54] The concept of immaterial labour was seen as particularly relevant to the fragmentary yet fluid demarcations between work and leisure in the lives of the employees, 'who consolidate office and home, who work and play in the same clothes, and whose social life draws heavily on their immediate colleagues', and, crucially, for whom 'there are no longer any boundaries between work and leisure'.[55]

In particular, over this period, artistic and creative labour were held to exemplify what Negri and others conceptualise under the banner of immaterial labour.[56] Manipulating symbols, attaching meaning to goods and services in pursuit of commodity exchange, and seemingly divorced in its content and setting from capitalist structures of 'evaluating and measuring labour', the work of the creative appears to lie 'beyond measure'. The crisis this precipitates, Böhm and Land write, is 'one of the central problematics of creative capitalism'—in short, 'how is the value of creative labour measured?' Part of the reason that creative labour threatens measurement in this way is its 'apparent autonomy', which, as it appears in the creative industries, acts for scholars of immaterial labour 'as a benchmark for other creative processes that seem to challenge the logics of industrial-capitalist organisation'.[57] Later, following the initial burst of interest in post-workerist approaches as a means to comprehend the rise of the Dot.Com boom and the so-called 'New Economy', newer strands of research focused, to a greater degree, on the rise of the internet and social media themselves as sites for the organisation of immaterial labour and the (co)production of immeasurable value.[58]

The uptake of post-workerism within studies of management and organisation has received wide-ranging criticism from other Marxisant strands of MOS, including from those who maintain adherence to the earlier forms of autonomist thought. In particular, the post-workerist depiction of a freely networked mode of production has been dismissed as 'wishful thinking' that converges with mainstream business theory in eliding the continuing relationships of control and dependence that characterise much of contemporary work.[59] By, for instance, simultaneously emphasising the 'value-creating potential' of brands whilst neglecting the global class relations on which capital valorisation rests, such approaches sometimes end up aligning critical organisational scholarship more with the image capital presents of itself than even mainstream economic analyses of the same empirical phenomenon.[60] Others have disputed the novelty of the 'free' labour on which post-workerism's focus falls, pointing to capitalism's dependence on the generation of a surplus by means of the exploitation of unpaid labour.[61] The claim of novelty rests, some suggest, on a masculinist fixation on the factory and its fortunes extended to apply to society as a whole.[62] From changes in the workplace, extended to fill society as a whole, much wider paradigm shifts are extrapolated. This ultimately productivist understanding of historical change is enthusiastically adopted irrespective of the continuities that characterise capitalist society, namely the persistence of forms of social domination resting beyond the workplace in the form of money, commodities and the state. In this light, post-workerism has been criticised for assuming that the self-valorisation of immaterial labour brings about the obsolescence of the law of value and the processes of capitalist control and measure it implies, when 'the vast bulk of knowledge workers can produce nothing without access to capital and without subordination to the wage relation'.[63]

In particular, an alternative route through these issues has been charted in the US and the UK by autonomists, sometimes in or at least adjacent to MOS, producing insights that bear a greater fidelity to post-workerism's 'workerist' precursor. The principal theorists of this strand include George Caffentzis, Harry Cleaver and Massimo De Angelis.[64] This strand of autonomism is defined by a 'strategic' or 'political' reading of Marx's critique of political economy (CoPE) that stresses the necessity of an active class struggle against value, conceptualised not as a positive quantity but a negative relation of domination.[65] Unlike post-workerism, this renewed appeal to core autonomist principles retains a focus on managerial control and measurement in the workplace, as well as the continuing relevance of worker struggle over how work is valued and measured.[66] Here, the 'affirmationism' of Negri's conceptualisation of the multitude's capacity to create the world in its own image is eschewed for the dynamic negativity with which the class antagonism was endowed in workerism originally.[67]

Owing to a belief that the kind of working conditions apprehended by first-generation workerism are a thing of the past, post-workerists claim that conventional organisation of labour is theoretically moribund and that socially necessary labour time (SNLT) is no longer the relevant measure for value in the conditions of immateriality characterising labour in contemporary capitalist society, with shifts in the qualitative and quantitative character of labour in the contemporary economy having rendered 'the relation between time and quantity of produced value' highly 'difficult to determine'.[68] However, autonomists who stress the workerist inheritance over the postmodern spin provided by post-workerism have sought to critique this articulation of the 'crisis of measurability', with one of the foundational contemporary contributions being the work of Caffentzis.[69] Caffentzis observes that 'the process of creating propositions, objects, ideas and forms and other . . . "immaterial products" . . . is a process in time that can be (and is) measured' just like any other, and that measurability endures the uncertainty post-workerism ascribes to it in any line of work.[70] Rather than value hinging on direct labour time, as post-workerist analyses imply, for autonomists, the social necessity of labour time is a measure to which labour is continuingly made subject in arbitrating its value-productiveness as abstract labour. As Cleaver writes,

> the concern with abstract labour (value) drives capitalists to shape the division, and hence the very structure, of useful labour in order to realize the homogeneity of abstract labour. Because of this, *useful labour in capital must be seen as the very material out of which abstract labour is crafted.* The work that is imposed on people through the commodity-form, which constitutes the substance of value in capital, exists only in the fluid structure of concrete useful labour.[71]

Such a perspective on the relationship between labour, measure and value has been articulated within MOS, namely in an intervention by David Harvie and Keir Milburn. That 'our creative activity as human beings—work—takes the form of value, of abstract labour' implies that labour is itself 'determined' by means of the category of value'. In this way, 'value organizes labour'.[72] Rather than calling measurement into question as stricken by a terminal crisis, as do post-workerist approaches, for these autonomist approaches, the measurements to which labour is subject in its abstraction as value are market-mediated and expressed in price, whilst keeping in view that 'value—market value—must be understood as emerging from relationships amongst people', and, moreover, that value, 'having emerged from human relationships . . . then turns around to domi-nate these relationships':

> the measures thus constructed (and imposed) are not passive. Within the organization, they are wielded as management tools to (re)organize—or *determine*—labour, i.e. 'to improve productivity and efficiency'. Out-side the organization, they are reflected in price levels, which, mediated by the competitive process and the market, influence—or determine—the organization of labour elsewhere in the economy. (The external market validates—or not—the organization and determination of con-crete labours within the organization.) As the McKinsey slogan puts it: '*everything can be measured and what gets measured gets managed*'.[73]

Examples of empirical areas to which an autonomist Marxist analysis of value, measure and class struggle have been fruitfully applied within MOS include waitressing, the use of metrics in academic labour, the creative indus-tries, and urban gentrification.[74] A central concept here is 'value struggles', reflecting the continuing antagonism characterising the attempts of capital to measure and value labour and the political subjectivities of the class actors who contest these attempts.[75] The concept of 'value struggles' relates to how productive human activity and its lived experience are abstracted through their quantification as wage labour, alienating the worker from work and its result and themselves, and how they might resist this alienation. For De Angelis, abstract labour has a practical existence as a particular kind of alienated activity over the content and result of which the worker has no control. Value is, in this understanding, nothing other than the 'analytical representation of the antagonistic class relation of work'.[76]

In an empirical study, De Angelis and Harvie use this conceptualisation to underpin an analysis of the measurement of so-called 'immaterial labour' in the UK Higher Education system by means of a plethora of metrics and standards. They point to the continuing relevance of the arsenal of tools deployed in Taylorist scientific management to measure, and thus manage, labour of an inscrutable or cognitive character like that found in academia. Under scientific management, collective knowledge was objectified in formalised processes within the workplace, wherein workers' situated 'knowledge of specific tasks'—'*how?, how much?, how long?, how many?*'—was 'appropriated' by managers as a tool of organisation and exploitation. Whilst simultaneously socialising worker knowledge, Taylorism represented a 'war over measure'.[77] The expansive understanding of bureaucratic or scientific management as a form of socialisation—bridging, in some ways, with the paleo-Marxism encountered in Chapter 2—offers an alternative way of understanding its applicability to contemporary 'immaterial' labour, which it 'shapes' just as effectively as it did 'material' labour in previous phases of capitalist production.[78]

Some of the empirical and theoretical criticisms and corrections of ideas of so-called 'immaterial labour' and the 'crisis of measurability' seem to have had a worthwhile effect on the development of post-workerist analyses of the relationship between labour and value. Noting the relevance of traditional forms of industrial organisation like scientific management to immaterial labour, in recent work, Hardt and Negri have used the concept of 'digital Taylorism' to explain how measure persists in spite of the underpinning crisis they have posited in previous work. Whilst 'absorbing cognitive labour', Hardt and Negri argue that Taylorism also translated 'exploited labour' into a 'mass opposed to command' with 'new technical knowledges' at its disposal liberated from within its 'subjugation'. Hardt and Negri take forward this analysis to describe contemporary labour, wherein they propose that coordination and performance become the autonomous and decentralised preserve of workers rather than management, struggling against absorption in new forms of 'digital Taylorism'.[79] In a stepchange from their earlier prognostications of a measurability crisis, Hardt and Negri stress that this situation need not imply that 'overflowing productive forces and the immeasurable values of the common sound the death knell of capital' itself, so long as technological developments 'domesticate immeasurability' and 'stamp values on the immeasurable'.[80] Whilst capitalist value and measure are challenged by the unruliness of the subjective basis of contemporary production, changes in the workplace do not simultaneously express the creative and communicative desire of workers, who are still 'exploited and worn down'. This newly pessimistic assessment of the situation reflects the exhaustion of the promise of the New Economy and its usurpation by the emergent gig economy.

In particular, a new workplace regime shaped by algorithms and platforms enables digital Taylorism to reinstitute scientific management and rendering previously hard-to-measure tasks measurable.[81] This technological fix confronts the resistance of contemporary immaterial labour to 'calculation, measure, and objectification'. Digital Taylorism, it is contended, temporarily suspends this not by pretending that 'all human and social phenomena are measurable', but rather by selecting only 'objective' data about work, setting aside the unquantifiable and autonomous 'subjectivity' that 'overflows and exceeds the objective measures stamped on it in the processes of capitalist valorization'. However, this places capital in the contradictory position of imprisoning the subjectivity of creative, social labourers within 'dimensions of industrial discipline' that run the risk of 'reducing productive powers and thwarting its own thirst for profit'—and hence the fundamental tension between capitalist technological development and the law of value is preserved, even as its countertendencies are subject to greater theoretical elaboration.[82]

Workerist MOS? New class cleavages in the social factory

The rise of digital Taylorism, and the responsiveness of post-workerists to it as they have revised their own over-optimistic appraisals of the direction of capitalist development, is indicative of how, as the once novel New Economy of digital and creative industries has passed over into the age of 'platform capitalism', some of the attraction of post-workerist analyses has waned with it. Interestingly, the rise of platforms has stimulated renewed interest in first-generation workerism and its conceptualisation of class composition.[83] In particular, this new wave of CCA examines key contemporary issues facing workers in a labour market and workplace refashioned around the platform or gig economy, especially for younger workers in the urban centres. The concept of class composition is here deployed to understand the emergent subjectivities of gig workers and other groups of workers perceived as characteristic of a changing economy.[84] This represents the latest version of workerism's attempt to locate a 'segment of the class . . . both dynamic in its behaviour, and employed in a sector of strategic importance'.[85] Workerists have found this segment in car factories, transportation and, later, in Bologna's 'second-generation autonomous work'. Post-workerists found it in students and youths performing 'immaterial labour'. Today's compositionists, meanwhile, find it in those subject to gig work in the platform economy, rented private accommodation and the financialised precariousness associated with young urban graduates. The cycle of struggles in the period following the financial crisis exposed this emergent social agent through city-street mobilisations that articulated diverse grievances by means of the same 'cybernetic technologies' that helped bring 'this new class composition into being'.[86] However, the apparent collapse of more conventional and coordinated modes of class struggle demands we reconsider how this incoherent generational and economic subjectivity can be politically organised in the context of 'the erosion of stable jobs, the use of digital technology to proliferate work tasks, the introduction of the precarious on-demand economy, the reinvention of Taylorism, [and] the massive financial and ideological power of tech companies'.[87] In this way, workerism—if not, perhaps, its post-workerist successor—provides a possible basis for new lines of theoretical and empirical enquiry in MOS.

In particular, the contemporary recuperation of the tools provided by first-generation workerism has witnessed a renewed focus on longstanding themes of compositionist analysis: youth, reproduction and the social factory, routed through a new generational politics matched to the age of the so-called 'asset economy' and 'rentier capitalism', concepts foreshadowed by earlier post-crisis (post)workerist contributions like Lazzarato's *Indebted Man*.[88] Here, we focus on two examples of the contemporary recuperation of workerist ideas of class composition within the broad disciplinary and empirical terrain of MOS: the analysis of 'social composition' developed by scholars and activist researchers in light of new organisational forms associated with the gig and platform economy; and the analysis of 'generation left' given by Keir Milburn.[89]

In their focus on the youth subjectivities unlocked by digital transformations in economy and society, the insights of these two strands of contemporary workerist-influenced organisational analysis can be read alongside Hardt and Negri's conceptualisation of the 'technical composition of the young'. In *Assembly*, Hardt and Negri revisit core workerist tenets and renew CCA in the context of contemporary left thinking about leadership and organisation in the wake of the failure of, first, post-crisis horizontalist politics and, later, the electoral turn associated with left populism. Hardt and Negri argue that the idea the technical composition determines political composition implies that 'workers can't represent themselves' and must instead be led by certain hegemonic fractions, imposing 'the hierarchies of capitalist production' onto political movements.[90] They propose that the 'post-industrial, digital and biopolitical' reshaping of work in the 1990s created a new relationship between 'the social composition of the labor force' and the 'technological composition of capital' that broke any such correspondence between production and politics. Instead, they suggest that capitalist command shapes society not through the employment relationship but as pure power over social relations epitomised in the corrupt 'benefits and privileges' appropriated by 'financial and propertied elites' against which the new class composition defined itself in movements that followed the 2008 crisis, albeit it only finding an effective organisational form in the left's more recent electoral turn.[91]

The workerist conceptualisation of the progression from technical to political composition, as Hardt and Negri observe, ultimately mirrored the orthodox Marxist progression from class in-itself to class for-itself. But today, the 'technical composition of the young', forged in 'biopolitical' production, practically refutes such a dialectical dualism between the material conditions of working life and the political composition of the class. In doing so, it refuses any institutional or organisational mediation or representation of its will such as that characteristic of prior compositions. Insofar as the workerist focus on labour is maintained, it is in the 'increasingly social forms' of 'immaterial production' from which value is extracted through financialised means across the full gamut of everyday life beyond the workplace.[92]

In this respect, for Hardt and Negri, the post-2008 protest and electoral movements show how the 'technical composition of the young generations' is no longer confined to production, nor to its precarious conditions, but encompasses a sociality and cooperation that renders the political composition always-already an aspect of the technical. This 'common' is taken to be most profound in all those sectors centring on the 'production of humans by humans'—'health, education, and various forms of service'. More broadly, 'the common (lived in social, productive and reproductive cooperation)' is experienced in production as well as constituting the 'political model of new institutions'. This 'common' thus comes to replace the traditional representative and mediated character of the relationship between technical and political composition, there effectively being no distinction between the politics of production and formal politics more widely.[93]

Contemporary production, and thus by extension contemporary class politics, centres, for Hardt and Negri, on a contest between, on the one hand, the young immaterial labourers who occupy the commons of social cooperation and represent the tendency of the technological forces to dissolve private property; and, on the other, the 'propertied elites' who extract surplus-value from the commons through financial means, reinforcing the existing relations of production. The opposition to inequality and austerity that characterised the post-crisis cycle of struggles, as well as new demands for a basic income commensurate to the commonwealth of cooperation, express the emergent conflict between this new technical-political composition and 'an old, unravelling political composition'.[94] As far as Hardt and Negri see it, the issue faced is the insufficiency of current property relations to properly recognise and accommodate the social and 'common' character of production. In the context of these property relations, Hardt and Negri pose the multitude as a productive majority ruled over by 'an extreme minority' that leeches upon the value they create.[95] In this, they follow contemporary political rhetoric in drawing sharp divides between productive and unproductive social actors:

> On one side are all those who live on the interest generated by the financial markets and seek to preserve exclusive access to the private property they accumulate. On the other side are those who produce social wealth through their collective knowledges, their intelligence, and their social capacities to communicate, care for, and cooperate with each other, who seek security through free and open access to the common they have produced. These are battle lines.[96]

In response to this 'battle', Hardt and Negri's recent work has expressed a marked shift from a politics based on the spontaneous resistance of the multitude to one based on its concerted organisation. Today, Hardt and Negri distance themselves from the 'refusal of all norms and organizational structures' and the resulting voluntaristic individualism, asking us instead to focus not on spontaneity itself but the structures and work that makes it possible—in other words, from 'changing the world without taking power' to a realisation that 'in order to change the world we need to take power'. The multitude appeared in their earlier work as an inchoate and limitless collective subject surpassing the narrow confines of proletarian class identity to encapsulate everyone and everything, whilst retaining the essential position of the proletariat in classical Marxist theory as an ontologically and epistemologically privileged revolutionary subject. Identified as the positive force driving capitalist development, post-workerism has typically placed few boundaries upon what could and could not be associated with the agentic energy of the multitude. However, as the hype of the New Economy and the new social movements that accompanied it subsides for an altogether bleaker global picture, the multitude 'designates a radical diversity of social subjectivities that do not spontaneously form together but instead require a political project to organize'. This means 'constructing the multitude "institutionally", that is, transforming the social experience of the multitude into political institutions'. In pursuit of this, Hardt and Negri are here unabashed in their recommendation of 'reformist action', with reform posed as a 'non-sovereign' alternative to revolutionary search for sovereign power. In this sense, there is still a residual commitment to an open politics of 'counter powers' dating back to first-generation workerist writings. The role of the counterpower this would establish would be to clear the way of obstacles to what Hardt and Negri describe as 'capacities for innovation'—returning to an idea common in this literature that there are potentialities awaiting to be unleashed were not for capitalist social relations.[97]

***

Hardt and Negri's collapsing of the distinction between the technical and the political composition is one of many attempts within the long history of (post)workerist CCA to revise and expand its boundaries. German autonomists Kolinko, for instance, propose to extend the analysis of worker subjectivity outwards from the workplace to the 'material conditions . . . of the relation of capital' as a whole, including the forms of reproduction specific to workers in a given labour process centring on the community, home, family and other institutions.[98] Inspired by this, the UK autonomist collective Notes from Below augment a dogged defence of the centrality of the workplace with a complementary perspective that transcends the workplace alone, represented in recent academic contributions within the broad area of MOS that connect inquiry with militant activity at the coalface of the gig economy.[99]

For this strand, whilst the traditional focus of workerism on the technical composition illuminates Marx's 'hidden abode' of production, its track record since the 1970s shows less success in analysing life 'beyond' the hidden abode. In conventional workerist composition analysis, Notes from Below observe, workers only come into focus outside the technical composition when they 'decide to act politically'.[100] When they are 'shopping, eating, relaxing or sleeping', meanwhile, workerism has tended not to be interested. However, the working-class constantly redefines its composition through struggles not only in the workplace but also 'beyond the wage' in spheres like social policy, rent, housing and consumption, which all represent instances of 'material organisation' just like those found in the labour process.

As such, an analysis of 'social composition' is required alongside the technical in order to apprehend the consequences both work inside the hidden abode and life beyond it imply for the development of workers' subjectivity in the political composition of the class. In the resulting model, the *technical* composition sees labour power organised into a working class, the *social* sees the organisation of the working class into a class society, and the *political* sees the self-organisation of that class into a 'force for class struggle'. The move from technical composition, through social composition, to political composition is characterised by what Notes from Below call a 'leap'. Just as 'through class struggle, capitalism changes itself', so too does the struggle introduce contingency into how the movement is made from the expansive terrain of technical composition to political composition. As Notes from Below acknowledge, 'Technical composition sets the basis for political composition, although the movement from one to the other is not mechanical or predictable'. The movement from one to the other by means of the 'leap' is the space in which 'the working-class political viewpoint' is formed.

Compositionists in this current stress the centrality of work as a guard against the post-workerist search for a succession of new social subjects 'everywhere but the workplace', and the attendant focus on vague instances of 'free labour' in the social factory at large.[101] In this sense, the suggestion of a focus on 'social composition' is by no means synonymous with an abandonment of the working class as an actor or agent of change. 'We need to analyse all aspects of working-class life', Notes from Below write. 'However, we think that abandoning work as the primary site of struggle is a mistake'.[102] Work is central for the likes of Notes from Below because the pivotal positions workers occupy in production and circulation grants them a privileged perspective.

However, although this privileged perspective is occupied 'intuitively', individual workers may struggle 'to see how their own work recreates capitalism every day' and thus require assistance in the form of the workerist approach of workers' inquiry.[103] The latter is proposed as a means to 'ground our politics in the perspective of the working class' whilst also decoding and representing the latter's experiences through the prism of class composition.[104] This method marks an extension of that utilised by the workerists insofar as the concept of social composition enables the analysis of 'the whole . . . working class', including the unemployed and those who work outside the production of commodities. Showing a continued political faith in the category of the working class, albeit it an expanded version, this analysis, they write, 'has to begin . . . from an exact and positive knowledge of the conditions in which the working class—the class to whom the future belongs—works and moves'. The leap towards social composition thus returns the working class to a well-worn historical mission.

Another compelling accompaniment to Hardt and Negri's focus on youth and Notes from Below's focus on 'social composition' can be found in Milburn's *Generation Left*, written in the context of the left electoral turn following the events of 2008–2011.[105] For Milburn, the 2008 crisis represents what Alain Badiou terms an 'event'—a 'moment of sudden and unpredictable change that rupture[s] society's sense making'—the effect of which was to define a generational composition assembling those worst affected by the recession and the deeper-lying political and economic tendencies it expressed. Drawing on the work of Karl Mannheim, Milburn suggests that due to a store of preloaded experiences prejudicing their capacity to react, older people will be slower to comprehend the consequences of such an event, whereas younger people carry a lighter load of memories and preconceptions, being therefore quicker to grasp the import of a given moment. The distribution of and divergence in these 'intellectual and psychic resources' at a point of crisis determine the separation of one generation from another. The political expressions of this in a given generational composition are not automatic, Milburn follows Mannheim in arguing, but rather cohere by virtue of attempts of vanguard 'generational units' to 'hegemonize the wider generation by providing "a more or less adequate expression of the particular 'location' of a generation as a whole"'.[106]

This 'intellectual and psychical' framework does not deliver us the whole story, however. For Milburn, 2008 was a case study in how different generations draw upon different *material*, as well as ideological, resources, in navigating the 'problem space' opened up by this 'formative event' which 'crystallised long-term trends of intergenerational injustice into a generation-forming period of change'. Milburn notes that this material terrain is conventionally addressed with reference to the concept of class, not age. But for Milburn, class is an increasingly meaningless framework insofar as the category of working class remains confined to an association with older skilled and manual workers, with younger service workers persistently codified as 'middle class'. This means also that class has all but become a 'proxy for age' in the terms used by pollsters and opinion-formers. At the same time, age has become 'one of the key modalities through which class is lived' and through which young people 'become aware of their actual class position'. Age also represents a 'fracture' that renders more difficult a cohesive account of 'mutual class interests', with younger people earning less, bearing more debt, having fewer job opportunities, and facing more barriers to home ownership than generations past.[107] The older property owners from whom they often rent, meanwhile, have seen their wealth soar in the post-crisis period, riding the wave of rising house prices. Like Hardt and Negri, Milburn characterises post-crisis capitalism as a story of elite appropriation of wealth through unconventional monetary policy, low interest rates and an asset price bubble, the benefits of which have accrued to older people.

The new salience of age does not undermine compositionist analysis but rather resonates with its theoretical and political roots in the struggle to comprehend and represent the 'problems and perspectives of a new generation of workers' in the 1960s, specifically the young 'mass workers' employed in factories such as FIAT Turin who prioritised work refusal over worker control.[108] However, in common with Hardt and Negri, Milburn sees the move from technical to political composition as having been complicated by the demassification, variegation and networkisation of work, as well as the displacement of antagonism from the production of value in the labour process, towards the extraction of rents in the circuit of capital as a whole. In the context of this 'complex and variable technical composition' incorporating the 'social composition' theorised by Notes from Below, 'thinking in terms of political generations and events' rather than class alone can help clarify the configuration of emergent political compositions.

Events illuminate 'which element has political valency' in a given composition, as 'generational units' stake their hegemonic claim to the definition and exploration of the 'problem space', these occurrences produce. In the present time, whereas 'the older generation are still tied to the neoliberal hegemony of finance', the 'young and disadvantaged . . . seek to escape it'. This rupture was clarified in the 'shared generational location' afforded first through the purely passive reception of the 2008 crisis and, second, the 'active' creation of an 'international left generation' in the horizontalist architecture of assemblies and consensus decision-making that characterised the 2011 'wave of protests and revolutions'. Rather than the events of the 'long 2011' having 'disappear[ed] behind the subsequent electoral turn' of the left, for Milburn, the latter represents their hegemonisation through organisational means better able to communicate with members of the same political generation less invested in activism. As such, contrary to Hardt and Negri's reading of the post-crisis horizontalist movements as a failure of organisational form, for Milburn, the increasingly 'cohesive fashion' through which generation left came of age politically—whereby the milieu behind Occupy London and the student movement led a 'take-over' of the Labour Party by the left in the UK—shows that they were actually a famous success.[109]

However, according to Milburn, these movements still confronted the difficulty of hegemonising or overcoming other age cohorts, with the political composition of generations as a modality of class ultimately determined by the desire of different actors for the upheaval or preservation of existing material conditions.[110] In this respect, Miburn follows Hardt and Negri in associating ownership of private property with *fear*—private property being central to a largely unachievable definition of adulthood, those who possess it perceived as jealously guarding it against those who do not.[111] In particular, Milburn identifies rentier dynamics as a particular site of de—and re-composition, insofar as 'the lives of the young are dominated' by various forms of rent extraction, whether in housing or the mediation of life and labour by platforms. This antagonism is 'shifting us from property-owning democracy to oligarchical rentierism', Milburn argues—a 'neo-feudalism' driven by the 'corruptive power of the oligarchs'.[112]

In a world where the thing 'oligarchs fear most' is 'raised consciousness', Milburn contends that the generational character of these economic shifts produces a new political composition based, somewhat innovatively in the historical context of CCA, on the left's turn towards formal parliamentary politics. Parliamentarianism's episodic character a poor fit for the 'temporality of movements', this composition implies that the left must reshape extra-parliamentary politics in order to keep 'Generation Left engaged enough to win the smaller electoral battles', whilst avoiding the subordination of all politics 'beneath the electoral party'. This is seen as a means by which the left can seize power to implement policies commensurate with the common and collective character of contemporary social (re)production, including, as in Hardt and Negri, a basic income. Whilst Milburn recommends the left sidestep a generational zero-sum game whereby the young rob the old of the assets, there is an urgent temporality driving this political recomposition insofar as 'the future can't afford' this generation's defeat.[113] As for Notes from Below, then, the future of the world rests upon the class actor produced by the current recomposition.

Class composition and the critique of political economy

These new approaches to understanding the relationship between the labour process and the valorisation process, and the politics of production and the politics of wider social transformations, represent a step beyond how Italian autonomist thought has been received in MOS to date. For autonomists that lean more towards an original workerist orientation, the positivisation of economic and social transformations presented by post-workerism means that the antagonism hardwired into the conceptual 'inversion' of class power slips from view, the course of capitalist development determined not through the struggle over or against labour, but through changes in labour itself. This has always been a risk within the Italian tradition from which these contemporary analyses derive their inspiration. Despite this risk, the return to an explicitly workerist CCA within and at the interstices of MOS and other areas of the critical social sciences has much to offer Marxist studies of work and organisation, eschewing the antagonism-free perspectives on 'immaterial labour' and so on that have pervaded the uptake of explicitly post-workerist analyses.

That said, that the return to workerism within the study of organisation can be critically comprehended through the prism of an alternative autonomist approach to core tenets of the CoPE. Emblematic of the continuing search for a class subject who chimes with the political aspirations of (post) workerism in its various guises, the identification of a new class composition springing from inequalities based on age, new forms of work and the rentierisation of assets reflects a longstanding tendency to focus on 'core' professional, cultural or geographical actors and sites of struggle owing to 'their significance in the social process of production'—beginning with FIAT Turin and ending with the digital labourers of today.[114] This has rightly served to expand the focus of activists and scholars beyond labour alone but has seldom upended the reductionism and vanguardism inherited from traditional Marxism. Whilst the most compelling contemporary accounts locate the conditions for the generalisation of struggles in sectors like logistics and delivery, for others, a crude fetishism of certain metropoles, generations and the kinds of precarious labour they incubate has come to stand in for any wider politics of work or value. The extension of the technical composition to include a greater array of social instances has simply shifted the location of material determination from the factory to the social factory—from one hidden abode to another—granting an ontologically and epistemologically privileged perspective to new groups and actors situated at alternative points of production without fundamentally challenging the orthodox logic of correspondence between the economic and the political.

This theoretical and rhetorical reflex has often concealed the absence of any practical know-how or means to generalise a given political composition. An exaggeration of the capacity of the struggles of certain metropoles, generations and kinds of labour to generalise themselves politically has come to stand in for any wider theorisation of the relationship between what LPT, as we saw in Chapter 2, calls 'the politics of production' and politics proper. Workerism arguably had 'too "pure" a view of the working class, leading to unrealistic . . . strategies' that rest on the presumption of an 'essential core' to its identity intrinsically 'against' capital. As well as eliding the role of culture and values in mediating and complicating the relationship between material conditions and political subjectivity, such an approach 'does not adequately recognise the degree to which "labour" as such is caught up in the commodity system' by virtue of the buying and selling of labour power, the working class occupying a position internal, rather than external, to the reproduction of capitalist social relations.[115] The strands of contemporary workerist-influenced organisational analysis considered here attempt to circumnavigate such a 'purist' conceptualisation of the working class through bridging to more expansive social terrain. Nonetheless, they are still characterised by the classical compositionist search for a straightforwardly antagonistic class subject whose interests are assumed to be diametrically opposed to those of capital, rather than a class subject constitutive of the capital relation itself.

Owing to this positivisation of antagonism, workerism and post-workerism display a tendency to 'homogenize' both blocs of workers and paradigms of capitalist production.[116] Their analyses of class composition respond to a perceived need to identify rising or hegemonic industries or economic conditions and place the workers or subjects who populate them at the forefront of programmes of political change and contestation. This consequently elides the heterogeneity of different kinds of work, worker and employment relationship within a given periodisation, and the diverse political and organisational expressions they assume. A focus on novelty in these homogenised paradigms and periods fails to account for continuities and 'holdovers' from before that would complicate the myopic identification of a single emergent class figure as the generational representative of the cutting-edge of capitalist development and the vanguard of the working class as a whole. The mass worker of the factories, the socialised worker of the cities and universities and the multitude of the digital and creative industries were categories analytically and politically as flawed as the understanding of the apparent paradigm shifts they represented, and it is likely the networked young worker in the gig or platform economy will face the same judgement. For workerist and post-workerist approaches to class composition, new economic paradigms periodically emerge to comprehensively wipe away the last without trace. But, in reality, they blend and coexist such that worker subjectivity can never be cleanly read off from material circumstances and, uncomfortably for compositionist analyses, carry traces of customs and traditions that are the residue of prior generational configurations. This has strategic implications for a contemporary left seemingly keen on a political coalition constructed around new kinds of work and workers—not least because CCA often serves to identify a central class subject whilst 'filtering out the rest' at the expense of an analysis of and appeal to the working class more broadly, including the resonance of culture and other factors.[117]

This search for new and decisive class actors, in eliminating contradictory and anachronistic elements, thus hypothesises recomposition where in fact *de*composition is as important a tendency.[118] Positivising capitalist development as always interconnected with class struggle obscures that its course is accompanied by a much more complex, and often politically unpalatable, array of manifestations of class subjectivity than workerism permits. Antagonism is treated as something waged between warring classes rather than something that 'traverses all of us' individually with unpredictable results—as, we shall see in the next chapter, it is understood by open Marxism, a critique and development of autonomist thinking. Moreover, antagonism cuts across classes themselves, insofar as class is temporarily fixed through myriad individual 'contracts between so many workers and so many employers' such that the relation between capital and labour is 'atomised and fragmented'.[119] In this way, processes of recomposition and decomposition are formed not only in the workplace but also in the interplay between the valorisation process and the labour process. Whilst this new current of autonomist MOS extends its focus beyond the workplace to this broader social totality, it does so only in an optimistic search for examples of recomposition where the labour process is lacking. This skirts the inconvenient truth of decomposition, whereby the progressive complexity of the valorisation process produces various 'intermediate strata' between capital and labour and separates 'secure wage workers' from the 'unemployed and immiserated'.[120] Different strands of workerism have traditionally attempted to overcome this complexity by theoretically articulating together the varied political behaviours of diverse social actors in a series of speculative theoretical and strategic gambits, from the mass worker to the multitude. But in doing so, their programmes of empirical and theoretical work have ended up 'flattening' the specificity of these actors and their behaviours to the detriment of analysis and thus praxis.[121] The danger is that contemporary attempts to revive workerist CCA produce similarly misleading theories that flow through into misguided organisational strategies.

Some strands of autonomist Marxism, in particular, reckon with this complexity by shifting the site of production or contestation to other social moments where divisions can be clarified. As part of this, they often displace antagonisms from the production of commodities and the appropriation of the value they bear, shifting it instead to the distribution of that value in the form of wealth. This can be seen in the increasingly distributionist direction taken in contemporary strands of CCA focused on the perceived power of wealthy propertied and financialised elites. The theoretical and strategic gambit of much contemporary analysis of class composition is that the key site where struggles are clarified today is not in production but distribution. This displaces the moment of material determination from work to another economic location, in particular financialised or rentierised processes of owning, leasing or speculating on the value of assets, which create new class compositions organised on generational or geographical lines. The earlier shift from the factory to the 'social factory' took a similarly distributionist bent. This reproduced the objective illusions through which productive relations appear in capitalist society, the fragmented and mediated character of class antagonism gaining coherence only by appearing as what it is not. The labour relation being formally mediated through manifold transactions between the buyer and seller of labour power in the sphere of exchange, its mode of appearance is not one of exploitation to be resolved at the level of the workplace, but an inequality between rich capitalists and poor workers to be resolved through distribution external to the workplace. Rather than a result of so-called 'false consciousness', this objective illusion underpins the reproduction of a society organised around the valorisation of value, and generates an internal opposition organised around distributionist critiques of the 'fragments' through which productive relations present themselves to us in the abstract form of rent, profit and their representative 'interest groups'. In indulging such appearances, contemporary (post)workerism runs the risk of providing a radical spin on the 'division, divide and rule' of bourgeois sociology, rather than the 'interconnection' between 'production and the way in which people relate to it, the relations of production' that characterises the theory of form presented in the CoPE.[122]

Understanding the valorisation process as being as much a crucible for recomposition and decomposition as the labour process has implications for how we evaluate attempts to extend the analysis of class composition to the sphere of circulation. The (post)workerist expansion of class composition from the factory to the social factory has tended to displace the 'hidden abode' of production onto new terrain rather than engage directly with the forms through which productive relations are mediated in exchange. This perspective is implicit in the power of material determination Hardt and Negri grant 'social cooperation' as the prevailing mode of value creation in contemporary capitalism. The new focus on assets, housing and finance among workerist-influenced organisational analysis, meanwhile, more capably captures how 'circulatory processes both rebound on and are shaped by the composition of classes', being both where labour power is bought and sold and 'where processes of credit, debt and speculation' take hold or come to a 'crashing halt'.[123]

However, this shift in the site of material determination not only fails to overcome the more fundamental problems identified by the above critiques of (post)workerism but also actually expresses their persistence. Class decomposition is a real dimension of the objective modes of existence through which capitalist social relations manifest themselves. This complicates attempts to 'imagine the working-class re-composition necessary to overthrow' those relations, leaving activists and intellectuals dissatisfied with the disappointing reality of working-class behaviour when confronted with the concrete conditions of work and life. This 'political impatience' leads to a constant pursuit of new class formations that can place revolutionary factions on the right side of emergent empirical and political tendencies. This process underpins the opening up of CCA to moments of the social totality beyond the 'immediate process of production' alone. However, in doing so, it tends to privilege as the most 'advanced' sector of the class those whose 'working-class behaviours' are culturally and politically closest to the radicals themselves.[124] At worst, the durability of the culture, tradition and history as mediating factors in the political behaviour of working-class subjects has led some militants to impose themselves or other social forces as a vanguard to help recompose the class by revealing to it the way the world really works. The strands of contemporary workerist-influenced organisational analysis charted earlier having been stimulated by the left's shift from structurelessness to structure in the so-called 'electoral turn', there is a risk that their development and reception is mediated through the new appeal of leadership to a left fresh from the experience of party politics, leading to the presumption that some form of external authority can impose coherence upon the contradictory elements of working-class life from outside.

The CoPE, however, tells us that class decomposition does not represent 'false consciousness' in action. Those subject to the relations of production cannot be ideologically or organisationally cleansed of the objective forms in which those relations really appear, because these forms are a necessary aspect of the social totality as a whole. Where the 'popular mind' does capture 'the interconnections between social phenomena' concealed in those forms of appearance, it is where the latter come into conflict with concrete experience. The antagonistic character of the productive relations these objective forms of appearance mediate means that the latter maintain an openness and lack of closure through which their interconnection can be momentarily clarified to those involved. This openness rules out the notion of revolution as an 'event' which abolishes or escapes a previously 'closed' system—such as that implied in Milburn's account of the 'moments of excess' experienced by 'generation left'—and reveals the system itself as fragile and open to change and struggle over its terms.[125]

Whilst a critical 'defetishisation' of social forms and the relations they mediate may help clarify the actual conditions for class recomposition, even on their own terms, many applications of compositionist analysis reinforce the fetishistic forms through which productive relations appear in their opposition to isolated fragments like 'rent' and their representative 'elites'. The practical consequence of the theory is thus inadvertently to compound class decomposition, as an intractable component of the same capitalist social relations concealed in these forms of appearance.[126] Meanwhile, contrary to the vanguardist temptation buried deep in workerism's orthodox Marxist past, workers require no hegemonic leadership to engage critically and practically with the social conditions before them, and the variety of political behaviours through which they express this, independent of material determination, should be treated as the starting point of left approaches to class politics rather than as a problem to be solved or avoided.

Conclusion

Among its critics, the spontaneist understanding of class struggle found across the various kind of autonomist Marxisms is characterised as imputing to workers an automatically and intrinsically antagonistic relationship with capital, when, in reality, this is mediated by a range of other phenomena and conditions that mitigate and channel the antagonism according to cultural, social and political factors. Whilst autonomism often successfully circumnavigates such a 'purist' conceptualisation of the working class, it still presumes an antagonistic class subject whose interests are straightforwardly contrary to those of capital. As the electoral ruptures of recent years have shown, the leap from material circumstances to political expression is rarely as direct or satisfactory to the hopes and aspirations of the radical left. Indeed, part of the 'autonomy' that human subjects have within capitalist society is precisely the capacity to act and think independent of material and economic conditions. Whilst the result of this autonomous capacity to decide sometimes disappoints radical theory, it should be treated as the democratic beginning point of any struggle for a better world

Whilst they display a tendency to simply displace the hidden abode of production as a point of determination onto other social phenomena, rather than truly illuminate what lies beyond it, the contemporary approaches charted in this chapter are undoubtedly a step in the right direction. Importantly, they hold implications both for theory and political practice, potentially opening up a more comprehensive understanding of antagonism—and thus of control, compliance and resistance—that reaches beyond common understandings and use of this concept in MOS. It moreover carries important political implications, as it enables envisioning struggle and solidarities across heterogeneous kinds of concrete labour, characterised by the spatio-temporal dispersion of production processes, and the increasing legal fragmentation of employment arrangements. Autonomist Marxism thus provides the basis to underpin analyses and strategies of class struggle that not only presuppose classical workplaces to be the 'natural' location where class struggles should originate—albeit an important one—but also consider other possible locations.

Notes

1   In places, this chapter draws upon Pitts FH (2013) A science to it: Flexible time and flexible subjectivity in the digital workplace. *Work Organisation, Labour & Globalisation* 7(1): 95–105; Pitts FH (2014) Time crisis. *Sociologia Del Lavoro* 133: 171–182; Pitts FH (2020a) Measuring and managing creative labour. *Organization*. doi:10.1177/1350508420968187; Pitts FH (2020b) The multitude and the machine. *Political Quarterly* 91(2): 364–372; Pitts FH

(2022) Contemporary class composition analysis: The politics of production and the autonomy of the political. Unpublished working paper.
2 Cleaver H (2000/1979) *Reading Capital Politically.* Edinburgh: AK Press, 129, 65.
3 Tronti M (2019/1972) *Workers and Capital.* London: Verso; Alquati R (2013) Organic composition of capital and labour power at Olivetti. *Viewpoint* 27. Available at: https://viewpointmag.com/2013/09/27/organic-composition-of-capital-and-labor-power-at-olivetti-1961/; Panzieri R (1976) Surplus-value and planning: Notes on the reading of *Capital.* In: *The Labour Process and Class Strategies.* CSE Pamphlet, No. 1. London: CSE, pp. 4–25; Bologna S (1976) Class composition and the theory of the party at the origin of the workers councils movement. In: *CSE Pamphlet No.1. The Labour Process & Class Strategies.* London: CSE, pp. 68–91.
4 CSE (1976) *CSE Pamphlet No.1. The Labour Process & Class Strategies.* London: CSE; Thompson P (2018) The refusal of work: Past, present and future. *Futures of Work* 1. Available at: https://futuresofwork.co.uk/2018/09/05/the-refusal-of-work-past-present-and-future/; Zerowork (1975) Introduction to Zerowork I. *Zerowork* 1. Available at: https://libcom.org/library/introduction-zerowork-i
5 Wright S (2014) Revolution from above? Money and class-composition in Italian Workerism. In: van der Linden M, Roth KH (eds.) *Beyond Marx.* Leiden: Brill, pp. 369–394 (369).
6 Wright S (2002) *Storming Heaven.* London: Pluto, 49, 78; Mueller G (2020) *Breaking Things at Work.* London: Verso, 15–16.
7 Wright 2002: 78.
8 Hardt M, Negri A (2001) *Empire.* Cambridge: Harvard University Press; Hardt M, Negri A (2004) *Multitude.* London: Penguin.
9 Hardt M, Negri A (2009) *Commonwealth.* Cambridge: Harvard University Press; Hardt M, Negri A (2012) *Declaration.* Argo-Navis.
10 Hardt M, Negri A (2017) *Assembly.* Oxford: Oxford University Press.
11 Bologna S (2013) Workerism: An inside view: From the mass-worker to self-employed labour. In: van der Linden M, Roth KH (eds.) *Beyond Marx.* Leiden: Brill, pp. 121–143; Bologna S (2018) *The Rise of the European Self-Employed Workforce.* Milan: Mimesis.
12 Englert S, Woodcock J, Cant C (2020) Digital workerism: Technology, platforms, and the circulation of workers' struggles. *tripleC* 18(1): 132–145 (134).
13 Steinhoff J (2020) *Automation and Autonomy.* New York: Palgrave, 75–97.
14 Wright 2002: 3–5.
15 Dyer-Witheford N (2015) *Cyber-Proletariat.* London: Pluto, 29.
16 Wright 2002: 3–5.
17 Wright 2002: 48–49; Alquati 2013.
18 Kolinko (2003) Class Composition. *riff-raff.* Available at: www.nadir.org/nadir/initiativ/kolinko/engl/e_klazu.htm
19 Cleaver 2000: 67.
20 Dyer-Witheford 2015: 29–30.
21 Wright 2002: 76–77; Mueller 2020: 128.
22 Wright 2002: 3–5, 78.
23 Mohandesi S (2013) Class consciousness or class composition? *Science & Society* 77(1): 72–97 (91–92).
24 Wright 2002: 138.

25 Wright 2002: 80.
26 Cleaver 2000: 70–71; Dyer-Witheford 2015: 30.
27 Cleaver 2000: 73.
28 Dyer-Witheford 2015: 37.
29 Mohandesi 2013: 92–93.
30 Wright 2002: 141, 163–164.
31 Wright 2002: 171–174, 201–202.
32 Bologna S (1979) The tribe of moles: Class composition and the party system in Italy. In: Red Notes (ed.) *Working Class Autonomy and the Crisis*. London: CSE.
33 Wright 2002: 207.
34 Boffo M (2014) From post- to Neo-: Whither operaismo beyond Hardt and Negri? *Historical Materialism* 22(3–4): 425–528 (428–434).
35 Hardt & Negri 2017: 173.
36 Hardt & Negri 2017: 37.
37 Hardt & Negri 2017: 81, 189.
38 Hardt & Negri 2017: xvi, 94.
39 Ross A (2003) *No-Collar: The Humane Workplace and Its Hidden Costs*. New York: Basic Books, 201.
40 Lazzarato M (1996) Immaterial labor. In: Virno P, Hardt M (eds.) *Radical Thought in Italy*. Minneapolis: University of Minnesota Press, pp. 133–150 (138).
41 Hardt & Negri 2004: 111–112.
42 Virno P (2004) *A Grammar of the Multitude*. LA: Semiotext(e), 102–103.
43 Lazzarato 1996: 140–141.
44 Pitts FH, Cruddas J (2020) *The Age of Immanence*. School of Sociology, Politics & International Studies Working Papers 01–20. Bristol: University of Bristol.
45 Marx K (1973) *Grundrisse*. London: Penguin, 704–706; Vercellone C (2007) From formal subsumption to general intellect. *Historical Materialism* 15: 13–36; Virno P (2007) General intellect. *Historical Materialism* 15: 3–8.
46 Vercellone C (2010) The crisis of the law of value and the becoming-rent of profit. In: Fumagalli A, Mezzadra S (eds.) *Crisis in the Global Economy*. New York: Semiotext(e), pp. 85–118.
47 Marazzi C (2008) *Capital and Language*. Los Angeles: Semiotext(e).
48 Willmott H (2010) Creating 'value' beyond the point of production. *Organization*. 36(4): 517–542; Beverungen A, Böhm S, Land C (2015) Free labour, social media, management. *Organization Studies* 36(4): 473–489; Arvidsson A (2010) The ethical economy: New forms of value in the information society? *Organization* 17(5): 637–644; Arvidsson A (2013) The potential of consumer publics. *Ephemera* 13(2): 367–391; Böhm S, Land C (2009) No measure for culture? *Capital & Class* 97: 75–98.
49 Terranova T (2004) Free labour. *Social Text* 18(2): 33–58; Beverungen et al. 2015; Böhm S, Land C (2012) The new 'hidden abode'. *Sociological Review* 60(2): 217–240; Arvidsson 2010: 640.
50 Willmott 2010: 521; Beverungen et al. 2015: 473; Terranova 2004.
51 Terranova T (2010) New economy, financialization and social production in the Web 2.0. In: Fumagalli A, Mezzadra S (eds.) *Crisis in the Global Economy*. Los Angeles: Semiotext(e), pp. 153–170 (155–156).
52 Hardt & Negri 2001: 402–403.
53 Terranova 2010: 153.

54 Ross 2003: 44–51.
55 Ross 2003: 19.
56 Böhm & Land 2009: 76–77.
57 Böhm & Land 2009: 94.
58 Arvidsson 2010, 2013; Beverungen et al. 2015.
59 Thompson P (2005) Foundation and empire. *Capital & Class* 86: 73–100; Thompson P, Briken K (2017) Actually existing capitalism. In: Briken K, Chillas S, Krzywdzinski M, Marks A (eds.) *The New Digital Workplace*. Basingstoke: Palgrave, pp. 241–263; Smith C, Thompson P (2017) Capital and the labour process. In: Schmidt I, Fanelli C (eds.) *Reading 'Capital' Today*. London: Pluto Press, pp. 116–137.
60 Willmott 2010.
61 Böhm & Land 2012; Zanoni P (2019) Labor market inclusion through predatory capitalism? In: Vallas S, Kovalainen A (eds.) *Work and Labor in the Digital Age*. Bingley: Emerald Publishing, pp. 145–164.
62 McRobbie A (2016) *Be Creative*. London: Wiley.
63 Adler P (2009) Marx and organization studies today. In: *Oxford Handbook of Sociology and Organization Studies*. Oxford: Oxford University Press, pp. 62–91 (71).
64 Caffentzis G (2013) *In Letters of Blood and Fire*. Oakland: PM Press; Cleaver 2000: 129; De Angelis M (2007) *The Beginning of History*. London: Pluto Press.
65 Cleaver 2000; Caffentzis 2013; De Angelis M (1995) Beyond the technological and the social paradigms. *Capital & Class* 19(3): 107–134 (128).
66 Harvie D, Milburn K (2010) How organizations value and how value organizes. *Organization* 17(5): 631–636.
67 Noys B (2012) *The Persistence of the Negative*. Cambridge: Cambridge University Press.
68 Arvidsson 2010: 637; Berardi F (2009) *The Soul at Work*. Los Angeles: Semiotext(e), 75.
69 Caffentzis G (2005) Immeasurable value? *Commoner* 10: 87–114; Caffentzis 2013; see also Pitts FH (2017) *Critiquing Capitalism Today*. New York: Palgrave, 199–201.
70 Caffentzis 2013: 111.
71 Cleaver 2000: 129.
72 Harvie & Milburn 2010: 631–632.
73 Harvie & Milburn 2010: 634–635.
74 Dowling E (2007) Producing the dining experience. *Ephemera* 7(1): 117–132; De Angelis M, Harvie D (2009) Cognitive capitalism and the rat-race. *Historical Materialism* 17: 3–30; Pitts 2020a; Frenzel F, Beverungen A (2015) Value struggles in the creative city: A people's republic of stokes croft? *Urban Studies* 52(6): 1020–1036.
75 De Angelis 2007; Frenzel & Beverungen 2015.
76 De Angelis 1995: 107.
77 DeAngelis & Harvie 2009: 4.
78 DeAngelis & Harvie 2009: 27.
79 Hardt & Negri 2017: 143, 188.
80 Hardt & Negri 2017: 213.
81 Hardt & Negri 2017: 131–132.
82 Hardt & Negri 2017: 143.

83   Indicative of the new uptake within MOS of workerism was an article forth-
     coming in *Organization Theory* made available ahead of print during the
     period this chapter was being completed, which promises to relate the con-
     cept of the 'social factory' to debates in organisation studies: Mumby DK
     (forthcoming) Theorizing struggle in the social factory. *Organization Theory*.
     doi:10.1177/2631787720919440
84   Cant C, Woodcock J (2020) Fast food shutdown: From disorganisation to
     action in the service sector. *Capital & Class* 44(4): 513–521; Englert et al.
     2020; Kearsey J (2020) Control, camaraderie and resistance: Precarious work
     and organisation in hospitality. *Capital & Class* 44(4): 503–511; Notes from
     Below (2018) The workers' inquiry and social composition. *Notes from Below*
     1. Available at: www.notesfrombelow.org/article/workers-inquiry-and-social-
     composition; Woodcock J (2014) The workers' inquiry from Trotskyism to
     Operaismo: A political methodology for investigating the workplace. *Ephem-
     era* 14(3): 493–513.
85   Wright 2002: 207.
86   Dyer-Witheford 2015: 150–151.
87   Mueller 2020: 128–129.
88   Adkins et al. 2020; Christophers 2020; Lazzarato M (2012) *Indebted Man*. Los
     Angeles: Semiotext(e).
89   Notes from Below (2018) The workers' inquiry and social composition. *Notes
     from Below* 1. Available at: www.notesfrombelow.org/article/workers-inquiry-
     and-social-composition; Milburn K (2019) *Generation Left*. Cambridge:
     Polity.
90   Hardt & Negri 2017: 17.
91   Hardt & Negri 2017: 64–65.
92   Hardt & Negri 2017: 65–66, 202–203, 238.
93   Hardt & Negri 2017: 238–239.
94   Hardt & Negri 2017: 238–239.
95   Hardt & Negri 2017: xvi–iii, 64–65, 94, 202–203, 238–239.
96   Hardt & Negri 2017: 175.
97   Hardt & Negri 2017: 7, 21, 69, 73–74, 133, 224, 256–259, 278, 289.
98   Kolinko 2003.
99   Woodcock & Cant 2020; Kearsey 2020.
100 Notes from Below 2018.
101 Englert et al. 2020: 135.
102 Notes From Below 2018.
103 Woodcock 2014; Pitts FH (2014) Follow the money? *Ephemera: Theory &
     Politics in Organization* 14(3): 335–356.
104 Notes from Below 2018.
105 Milburn 2019.
106 Milburn 2019: 19–21.
107 Milburn 2019: 21–23.
108 Milburn 2019: 24–26.
109 Milburn 2019: 30–31, 79–80, 87.
110 Milburn 2019: 82–83.
111 Milburn 2019: 108.
112 Milburn 2019: 115–116.
113 Milburn 2019: 120–124.
114 Kolinko 2003.

115 Dyer-Witheford 2015: 31.
116 Mohandesi 2013: 88–89.
117 Kolinko 2003.
118 Holloway J (2002) Class and classification. In: Dinerstein AC, Neary M (eds.) *The Labour Debate: An Investigation Into the Theory and Reality of Capitalist Work*. Aldershot: Ashgate, pp. 27–40; Wright 2002: 224.
119 Holloway J (1992) Crisis, fetishism, class composition. In: Bonefeld W, Gunn R, Psychopedis K (eds.) *Open Marxism II: Theory and Practice*. London: Pluto, pp. 145–169 (154); Holloway 2002: 46.
120 Dyer-Witheford 2015: 28–29.
121 Wright 2002: 224–225.
122 Holloway 1992: 154–155.
123 Dyer-Witheford 2015: 81–82.
124 Wright 2002: 224–225.
125 Holloway 1992: 156–157.
126 Holloway 1992: 156–157.

4 Behind the hidden abode

From primitive accumulation to the metabolic rift

Introduction

Thus far, we have delved *into* the hidden abode of production by means of Labour Process Theory's analysis of managerial control between the labour process and the valorisation process; and travelled 'beyond' the hidden abode of production accompanied by a range of autonomist Marxisms and their approaches to labour, value and class struggles. In this chapter, we look *behind* the hidden abode of production to understand its constitution in four categories or processes that, in many cases, have been left surprisingly neglected in many Marxist analyses, but which bridge to some of the core areas of interest compelling Management and Organisation Studies (MOS) scholars today: class and the state; gender and the sphere of social reproduction; racism and its historical and present-day connection with capitalism; and the environment, including humankind's conflicted metabolic relationship with nature.

In the first section of the chapter, we examine open Marxism, a critique and development that 'opens up' underlying autonomist themes introduced in the previous chapter by posing an alternative reading of the relationship between labour, value, class struggle and the state. Open Marxism helps recover an idea of class relations as determining a shared condition of social existence that originates *prior* to the utilisation of labour power in capitalist production process located in the workplace, and further extends its effects *beyond* it, in the actualisation of value in circulation through commodity exchange and the mediation of antagonisms in the form of the state.

In the second section, we explore Marxist-feminist approaches to the understanding of gender and processes of social reproduction—a set of perspectives that we follow other scholars in calling Social Reproduction Theory (SRT). We chart the twin focus of SRT upon the role of women in a gendered and racialised global division of caring labour, and the central position this labour plays in the reproduction not only of workers in

DOI: 10.4324/9781003198895-4

capitalist society but also of capitalist society itself. This redresses the one-sided focus of traditional Marxism upon the politics of class alone by opening out the critique of political economy (CoPE) to other moments of social domination, antagonism and subjectivity. The utility of the approach is demonstrated through a case study of the valorisation of different kinds of labour power in crowdsourcing platforms, and the role played by state policy in supporting their reproduction, before considering some the alternative forms of social reproduction proposed by activists, theorists and social movements.

In the third section of the chapter, we map approaches to the political economy of racial capitalism drawn from Black Marxism, which focus on the relationship between slavery and labour, the role of primitive accumulation in the constitution of capitalist society, and the significance of the state in mediating antagonistic social relations. We demonstrate the usefulness of this framing of management and organisation using a case study of the political economy of policing and incarceration in the United States. We also, here, relate the critique of antiblackness to the critique of antisemitism found in some strands of critical Marxism, exploring the relationship between these two distinct and specific forms of racism in terms of their relationship with the social relations and social forms that structure and govern work and economic life.

In the fourth section, we consider the relevance of Marx's CoPE to the understanding of environmental crisis, charting the development of ecological Marxism as a way of understanding the human 'metabolism' with nature and the crisis sparked by the 'metabolic rift' caused by its human transformation. We consider how organisational scholars have begun to deploy concepts from ecological Marxism to consider valorisation processes around natural resources, and in particular waste. A case study of labour in the circular economy is used as an example of how this theoretical perspective can illuminate contemporary issues of concern in management and organisation. We then close by delineating coordinates for the possible alternatives those new directions in Marxian MOS can help us conceptualise within and beyond contemporary capitalist society and the forms of labour and value that characterise it.

Open Marxism: class and social constitution

So-called 'open' Marxist approaches to class struggle and social policy derive from the same debates about money, crisis and the state in and around the Conference of Socialist Economists in the UK in the 1970s and the 1980s that introduced Anglophone Marxism to the workerism discussed in the previous chapter. Open Marxism in many ways represents a continuation of autonomist themes combined with an elaboration of aspects of Marx's CoPE reconfigured to encounter new theoretical and empirical terrain. Its key thinkers include Werner Bonefeld, Simon Clarke, Ana Dinerstein, Richard Gunn and John Holloway, whose individual contributions are represented in a defining book series beginning in the 1990s and revived with a recent new instalment.[1] The work of these thinkers engages with key concepts of Marx's CoPE: the value-form, abstract labour, commodity fetishism and the socially significant role played by money in capitalist society.[2] But its shared foundation in Marxian form analysis goes much further in 'seeking to reveal the human content of formal economic categories' by unveiling their social constitution in the 'actual relations' of life in class society.[3] Inspired by Adorno's *Negative Dialectics*, open Marxism exposes the 'non-conceptuality' concealed, denied but nonetheless carried over within the 'conceptuality' of the quantitative abstractions in which social domination in capitalist society is moored.[4] Contrary to the traditional Marxist 'base-superstructure' approach, open Marxism does not attempt to strip away social forms like value as a kind of false appearance overlaid upon material reality. Rather, it enquires after what is contained within such social forms, as the objective 'modes of existence' social relations assume in thought and practice under capitalism. On the basis of this reading, forms such as value, money, the wage and the state represent the temporary and unresolved mediation of the intractable contradictions central to the antagonistic social relations constitutive of capitalist society.[5] In search of the grounds of this social constitution, open Marxism goes behind the hidden abode of production to begin unpicking the historical and continuing conditions that make it possible at all.

In doing so, open Marxism rethinks class beyond the narrowly distributionist and economistic definition into which the autonomist analyses discussed in the previous chapter sometimes veer. For open Marxism, the unequal distribution of wealth and property along class lines is not a simple outcome of competing class interests or a result of capitalist development but foundational to the whole structure of capitalist society—a precondition of wealth itself in the form we know it. The equivalent exchange of labour for a wage, and of commodities for money, has its basis in the pursuit of profit by way of *unequal* exchange. This unequal exchange is predicated on, and not simply the result of, a classed society. In this way, open Marxism follows Adorno in understanding society as 'antagonistic from the outset' rather than as a consequence or condition of capitalist development in specific social and historical circumstances. It is necessary to understand objective economic categories like value containing within them their antagonistic social constitution in struggles over labour power, class, surplus-value and the separation from independent individual and collective means of living and subsisting. Valorisation is predisposed upon the pursuit of profit, which is predicated on inequality rather than inequality being its result.[6] This inequality 'structur[es] the lives of different individuals in different ways', establishing often contradictory identities and positions both across groups and as a 'fracture-line' running through individuals themselves.[7]

In its economic sense as the central social category of capitalist society, capital is not something competed over by class interests. Rather, the cleaving of society according to class is the very precondition of capital itself and the form of wealth it assumes in value.[8] Class is central to this in that profit 'entails the class relationship between the buyer of labour power and the producer of surplus value as seller of labour power'.[9] Similarly, class does not simply 'amount to the wage relation', but rather itself 'subsists through the wage relation'.[10] Class is a negative condition of conflicted interdependence. Workers depend upon the sale of their labour power to subsist, and the successful validation of their labour power as value-producing in the exchange of the goods and services in order to reproduce their conditions of continued employment. For this employment, they must compete against other workers in labour markets that are 'gendered, racialised, and also nationalised'.[11] Hence, class is an antagonistic and contradictory social relation that bestows no 'historical privilege' upon any given class subject, but exists always chafing 'in and against' the logical and historical conditions of its social constitution.[12] It is a story of *dispossession*, constantly reinforced through an ongoing process of primitive accumulation.[13]

This primitive accumulation is not something of the distant past, but a continuing state of affairs that must always be reproduced. For open Marxism, primitive accumulation is not a temporary or contingent phenomenon associated with a specifically imperialist form of capitalism, but rather a precondition for capitalist society itself, continually reproduced in the separation of workers from the means of subsisting independent of the commodification of the one use-value left at their disposal—their capacity to labour. This renders one class dependent on the social forms through which its labour attains validity, and capital dependent on the validation of that labour for its own reproduction in turn. Thus, open Marxism adds flesh to the theory of the value-form found in Marx insofar as we materially subsist through and by means of mediations of a fundamentally abstract and social character. These forms—value, money and wage—mediate the class antagonism that sits, historically and logically, at the 'non-conceptual' core the 'negative dialectics of economic objectivity' unpicks from their abstract 'conceptuality'.[14] Open Marxism thus explores how capitalist social forms act as 'modes of existence' through which class antagonism is mediated.[15] Social mediation, in this context, describes the succession of intermediate forms that grant a mode of existence to the relationship between two or more other things, like a 'rope linking two climbers' constitutes the 'relation in which they stand'.[16] To this extent, forms of social mediation, like value, become the active mode of appearance assumed by the things they mediate.

The 'perverted' forms of mediation, such as value, money, the wage and the state, in which 'sensuous human practice' appears stand above and apart from the humans who perform the practice that produces them.[17] In this way, characteristic of open Marxism is the expansion of the frame of form analysis developed by Marx to comprehend value in *Capital* to include among the forms it studies those assumed by other moments of capitalist social life. This expansive analysis of social forms displaces the locus of domination from the class antagonism conceived solely in the context of the employment relation to a wider terrain of social reproduction and commodification occupying the social sphere as a whole.

Specific attention is paid to the state as one such form. Open Marxism understands the state not as a neutral instrument to be wielded by this party or that so as to spur or tame capitalist dynamics, but rather as itself a capitalist state, as a historically specific mode of existence assumed by the class antagonism.[18] For open Marxist approaches, class struggle moves 'in and against' the state to achieve legal and regulatory gains through the conditions of 'political integration' it offers the working class.[19] In this way, forms of social mediation like value and the state retain an openness owing to the social conflicts they carry over, which whilst expressed 'in the mode of being denied', grant struggles 'room to move'.[20] The state as a form of social mediation thus does not resolve the contradictions in which it is founded but preserves the space in which they play out. The persistence of struggles highlights how capitalist social relations and social forms do not simply 'come about and maintain [themselves] just like that' and are 'neither given nor assured', but rather characterised by and contingent upon struggle.[21] The inherent instability of capitalist social mediation 'signals its openness to a future' that is not necessarily contained within the range of possibilities its current reality permits.[22] This invites some open Marxists to stress the possibilities of *de*mediation that inhere not only 'in and against' but also 'in, against and *beyond*' the mediation enforced through abstract social forms of capital and state.[23] Open Marxism sees demediation as occurring where capitalism momentarily 'cracks', through small, isolated and sometimes overly individualised interventions into or abstentions from the reproduction of capitalist social forms like value.[24] Class struggle is then the context for prefigurative 'experimentation' with non-capitalist futures and the practices that will constitute them.[25] Importantly, demediation is not synonymous with pure immediacy, which, contrary to the likes of Hardt and Negri encountered in Chapter 3, is impossible in a world that subsists and is reproduced through mediations like value.[26] Rather, it gestures towards an analysis of antagonism where opportunities for alternatives might be found within the fabric of social mediations, rather than from a space of moral and political purity sitting somewhere outside it.

However, we might also see the state not as a form within which antagonisms play out in the open manner these approaches suggest, but as a space of closure by no means confined to societies where the state exerts an authoritarian hold on individuals and limits their free association. One specific dimension analysed by the Frankfurt School tradition of critical theory that open Marxism draws upon was the capacity of the state to fix in place the social relations of production when threatened by the unfolding technological forces of production. Other approaches we have considered here—such as paleo-Marxism in Chapter 2—have seen this dialectic as dynamic and full of movement, but it can have a 'static side', as Adorno puts it. Even though the forces of production might render the relations of production 'objectively anachronistic' or 'debilitated, damaged and undermined', still they persist, largely because they 'no longer function autonomously'. The state steps in to superintend, 'summoned . . . to assist the intrinsic dialectic of society, which . . . would otherwise collapse'.[27] Here, the state comes into its own as the primary 'means of containing social antagonism'.[28]

In this way, the critical tradition within which open Marxism stands shines a light on how economic and organisational relationships cannot always be conceived of as flowing neatly from rational material bases. For Adorno, for instance, seeing the forces of production accomplishing changes in the relations, traditional Marxism here 'presupposed' precisely the same 'undisturbed, autonomous running of the mechanisms of the economy postulated by liberal theory'.[29] This ignores the function of social and political power in determining the unfolding of technological and economic forces. The state in particular specialises in schemes of 'extraeconomic' support that ultimately satisfy 'the system's consciousness of the conditions that enable it to be perpetuated'.[30] As Adorno puts it,

> the ruling class is so well fed by alien labor that it resolutely adopts as its own cause the idea that its fate is to feed the workers and to 'secure for the slaves their existence within slavery' in order to consolidate its own.

It is a happy consequence that, in doing so, it secures also the subsistence and social reproduction of the worker—the human who subsists as labour power—within the same system.

Touching upon key areas of interest to contemporary organisation scholarship, an open Marxist understanding of class struggle and its fluid relationship of contestation within and against the state has been applied by Ana Dinerstein in a study of how the Argentinian 'Unemployed Workers

Organizations' (UWOs), an array of autonomous social movements, mobilised 'in, against and beyond' the state in the wake of the economic crisis that hit Argentina at the turn of the millennium. Nicknamed the '*piqueteros*' for the roadblocks they erected in protest, these movements leveraged collective resources from the state, such as unemployment benefits and welfare payments, to autonomously and collectively recreate the world of work and reconstruct their communities. They started cooperative projects to build homes, establish community farms, and create job agencies. Some UWOs went further and took on political responsibilities unperformed by the state, acting as 'quasi-city councils' for the geographical areas they represented. This enabled them to institutionalise an open process of contestation and negotiation where state resources and social programmes were re-appropriated for collective purposes. Combining manifestations like roadblocks and new forms of local and municipal governance, the UWOs 'us[ed] resistance as a conduit for community development and community development as a conduit for resistance'. They translated autonomous mobilisation into 'welfare policy from below' that de-individualised welfare and recollectivised work in the pursuit of human dignity.[31]

In doing so, these movements offered an alternative to contemporary policy experiments like the universal basic income or local currencies, which claim to 'overcome the alienation inherent in the money form' through the capacity to 'rob money of its status and privileges' and in doing so solve the 'evils of capitalism'. Such monetary interventions—as we have seen, supported by post-workerists like Hardt and Negri—merely represent what Neary and Taylor call a 'fetishized and mystified reaction to the alienating conditions of the money-form', based in the 'reinvention of communities' on the basis of locality. As a '(re)negotiation of value' on a purely interpersonal level, in a futile fight against the distorted global rationality of financialised money flows, these forms of fairer money resist the 'totalising impact of money', but mistake the latter as purely a 'symbolic medium of exchange' to be 're-rationalised' in association with the 'real economy' it mediates. Fashionable experiments like local currencies therefore constitute an attempted 're-moralisation' of commodity exchange in search of a community and an ethic of equivalent exchange that is by definition impossible in capitalist society, where money is 'a generic representative of the property relation'. As Neary and Taylor write, 'the commodification and monetisation of society increases the dependence of individuals on the money-form through the way in which time and money become increasingly interlinked'. In a context of 'mechanisation of low-skilled labour-intensive work [and] the commodification of leisure', then, purely monetary social policy responses to the malaise of modern working life 'may thus serve to further exclude individuals on the margins of society'.[32]

According to Neary and Taylor, 'The limits of the struggle against money is that money is just the perceptible appearance of the contradictory social relations of capital'.[33] It is, therefore, these contradictory social relations that must be addressed. In this spirit, the Argentinian social movements Dinerstein describes did not simply seek to receive money in lieu of practical alternatives, but worked through the money-form to address its 'material determinations and historical context'.[34] In creating new mediations of their activity in, against and beyond the money- and state-forms, these movements thus centred on a productive tension between the 'affirmation of autonomy' in social movements' resistance against the state and the 'recuperation of autonomy' in their integration into the state.[35] The translation of social movement practices into policy could not erase their 'excess', paving the path for alternatives *beyond* the state and money altogether. This example is suggestive of what Dinerstein calls 'concrete utopias' as a focus for empirical research and political speculation.[36] This calls for research that focuses on existing human practices of building practical, feasible alternatives that work within the contradictions that are mediated in extant institutions of society and state. In examining such practices, within the context of critical MOS, research would explore the extent to which such struggles have the capacity to point beyond capitalist mediations. Such 'moments of excess' arise because the total subordination of human practice to its mediation by capitalist social forms is undermined by 'creative contradictory practice' taking hold at the 'interstices' of the antagonistic movement contained within mediation and its forms. The site for analysing and investigating antagonisms thereby becomes wherever these spaces of incomplete subordination—or 'cracks'—might be expanded in, against and beyond the forms of mediation through which humans subsist in capitalist society, such as money and the state.[37]

Marxist-feminism: gender and social reproduction

Open Marxism's focus on the social constitution of capitalist society in antagonistic relations of social reproduction and primitive accumulation is extended in Marxist-Feminist scholarship that similarly seeks to peer behind the hidden abode of production and uncover its historical and material conditions and determinants. Particularly of interest in this regard is SRT, a strand of Marxist-feminism that foregrounds the activities that biologically and socially reproduce labour power.[38] This includes 'the provision of food, clothing, shelter, basic safety, and health care, along with the development and transmission of knowledge, social values, and cultural practices and the construction of individual and collective identities'.[39] SRT departs from traditional Marxism's focus on workplace relations, which tends to take the 'existence of living individuals' for granted and see the elimination of classes as sufficient for the liberation of women from the unequal burden of sustaining life.[40] This approach instead addresses the 'conditions of possibility of labour power' which ensure workers are able to enter waged work in the first place.[41] This rests in the insight that labour power is a peculiar kind of commodity constituted in continuing processes of primitive accumulation that deprive workers of any other means of subsistence and deliver the worker to capital even before the latter has contracted the former to work.[42] For those who have no other independent means but to live and subsist as the personification of the one commodity they possess—labour power—life becomes mediated by the wage, commensurate with the reproduction of the worker and any dependants.[43] This understanding is grounded in the key observation that labour power is the only commodity that is not directly created through a capitalist process of production, but is rather reproduced through 'extensive, undervalued, and largely invisible' work occurring in communities, schools, hospitals, and religious and civil society organisations.[44] This rests on waged and unwaged formal and informal work disproportionately performed by women, often migrants or racialised subjects in a global division of labour.[45]

Marxist-Feminism in general, and SRT in particular, emerged as a distinct theoretical tradition in the early 1970s. Socialist feminists initiated an international debate on domestic labour, attempting to locate the socio-material foundations of women's oppression through the conceptual tools of Marxian political economy and casting women's work in the household as an object of critical inquiry.[46] SRT can be broadly divided into two complementary strands. A first strand centres on the role of women's unpaid reproductive work in the domestic sphere, female subjectivities produced by capitalism, and how gender relations within the working class ensure capital accumulation.[47] This strand of thought has known a new impetus after 2008, when the global financial and economic crisis came to be reconceptualised more fundamentally as a crisis of care and social reproduction under neoliberal capitalism.[48] A second strand, while acknowledging the historically specific role of women's and other subordinate social subjects' historically specific role in social reproduction, aims at extending Marx's theorisation of capitalism as such, in a way that adequately accounts for the social reproduction of labour power as its condition of possibility.[49]

The relation between patriarchy and capitalism was previously theorised by socialist feminists as a 'dual system', unintendedly reproducing an understanding of women's oppression as a mere addition to the 'core' of Marxism.[50] Meanwhile, from the 1980s onwards, many feminist intellectuals moved towards post-structuralist and post-modern theories, and increasingly conceptualised patriarchy as a symbolic, discursive, cultural and ideological phenomenon, dismissing not only materiality but also Marxism altogether, while feminist activism retrenched in many countries under neoliberal political pressures. Going beyond these tendencies, social reproduction theory poses the bigger question of how society organises the maintenance of the totality of labourers through the reproduction of life in the form of the commodity labour power. Social reproduction scholars agree that capitalism rests on unwaged labour in the domestic sphere and that it shapes life well beyond the sphere of production. Under capitalism, women's unpaid reproductive services in particular are necessary to continuously 'mend' men—physically, emotionally and sexually—in the home, to reproduce them as deployable labour power and enable their exploitation by capital in the workplace. The figure of the housewife is a cornerstone of these analyses.[51] The housewife—independent of whether she also engages in wage work outside the household—comes to epitomise a specific femininity, a naturalised essence of women as inherently docile, subservient and naturally caring of others rather than attending to her own desire, which crucially obscures the fact that reproductive work is work, and, just like work in the sphere of production, is alienated and exploited.[52]

But more broadly, this approach theorises oppression beyond the specific position of working-class women in processes of capital valorisation. The unpaid work not only of housewives but also of slaves, colonial subjects, prisoners, and other oppressed groups allows capital to contain the cost of labour power.[53] In this sense, contrary to analyses of capitalism focusing solely on the workplace and theorisations of class struggle as enacted by the waged workforce, SRT conceives of capitalist relations through the wage as constitutive of all other kinds of social relations under capitalism and, accordingly, of class struggle as potentially occurring in various locations. The emphasis on the multiple forms oppression takes under capitalism, next to and together with gender relations, sets the stage to conceptually integrate other relations such as race relations in a social reproduction critique of capitalist political economy, as we will explore in the next section. The variability and indeterminacy of labour power in this context makes social reproduction a key site of class struggles, expansively conceived. To expand, capitalism needs labourers to have new needs that can be satisfied by commodities, but must limit those needs to extract surplus value. In this sense, a social reproduction framework strategically locates class struggle at the intersection of the workplace and other spheres, incorporating, for instance, the fight for access to resources such as clean water, health services or education, and the rethinking of the articulation between class struggles and gender, race and geography.

In this focus, SRT extends and expands key concepts of Marx's CoPE, including the commodity, value, money, capital, labour power and surplus-value. For these analyses, the sphere of social reproduction reflects a contradiction at the heart of capitalism between the minimisation of the wage in pursuit of capital accumulation and the requirement to provide workers a wage which is sufficient to reproduce the labour power necessary for future capital accumulation. This contradiction became particularly apparent in the wake of the 2008 financial and economic crisis, which also highlighted how, in the shadow of crisis, individuals and communities search for alternative ways of socially reproducing themselves and others. In the wake of the retrenchment of the welfare state under austerity, empirical studies informed by SRT examine struggles over the domestic reproduction of labour power in the absence of collective services provided by the state or civil-society institutions; or commodified services employing migrant, racialised and female wage labourers to perform reproductive tasks.[54]

In this way, SRT also stimulates visions of social transformation and practical alternatives to address some of the issues it highlights. Starting from a Marxist analysis of the gendered nature of labour and reproductive labour influenced by ideas of the Italian workerist movement, the anticolonial movement, the student movement and the civil rights movement, Mariarosa Dalla Costa, Selma James, Brigitte Galtier and Silvia Federici launched the International Wages for Housework Campaign for the recognition and collectivisation of women's unpaid reproductive work in the household.[55] The claim for a wage for reproductive work was grounded in the idea that, by reproducing labour power, such work produced surplus value.[56] For instance, the International Wages for Housework Campaign's struggle for a wage for women's reproductive work was seen as a necessary political act towards the recognition of its value which will, in turn, allow for the recomposition of class interest which capitalism fragments along gender lines.[57]

Despite rising MOS interest in SRT, at the time of writing, only a few studies have adopted it.[58] The potential of SRT to broaden our understanding of value and class struggle is well illustrated by Patrizia Zanoni's study of the so-called 'sharing economy', critically interpreting the business model of platform-based firms relying on crowdsourced labour, such as Uber, Deliveroo and Amazon Mechanical Turk.[59] These companies fail to pay a living wage to the labour they crowdsource, offering extremely casualised work often through 'false' self-employment, piece rates and a lack of employee benefits. These employment conditions below subsistence are examined in relation to EU and national policies advancing crowdsourced work as a strategy to 'activate' historically subordinated groups who are underrepresented in the labour market—such as (ethnicised) youths, (female) individuals with caring responsibilities in the home, rural workers, individuals with disabilities and individuals in the Global South—through more 'flexible' working arrangements. The study reconstructs the diffuse yet consistent policy discourse casting platforms as key instruments to create more inclusive labour markets for a global, 'diverse' labour force.

In Zanoni's study, SRT helps frame crowdsourced labour as valuable for companies, because it is 'astoundingly cheap'.[60] This low cost is explained by reference to the historical inability of the most vulnerable workers to command access to work at living wages. Crowdsourcing institutionalises the inequality in the basket of goods workers can, at the intersection of class relations with patriarchy, ableism and racism, legitimately aspire to acquire in order to reproduce themselves.[61] The value of their labour is determined by the wage they are able to command for living, with most forced to lower their 'standard of necessity' to a minimum, and to rely on other sources of income to survive.[62] Importantly, the analysis advances existing studies of the gig economy by pointing to how the costs for reproducing labour are externalised not only to the individual worker but also to the state, through the welfare system, and ultimately, other segments of capital.

The study highlights the importance of expanding research to include struggles for social reproduction spanning the workplace, the domestic sphere and public policy and institutions. An analysis of the circuits of capital and social reproduction is key to unveiling how value mediates social relations, inscribing them along 'identity' lines, and to highlighting capitalism's contradictions as locations for class struggle. Importantly, SRT analytically de-individualises the social reproduction of life, taking it outside the realm of the individual worker's private sphere, and foregrounding the key role of the state (e.g. activation and labour market deregulation, migration policies, and childcare and health services) in setting the conditions under which labour power can be reproduced. In doing so, it expands the analytical horizon of MOS engagements with antagonism in capitalist society.

Black Marxism: race and primitive accumulation

Further expanding this analytical horizon in the study of antagonisms, Black Marxism interrogates the neglect or, at best, the 'cursory treatment of racial violence' by Marxists of all stripes, reflecting a narrowly class-based frame of analysis in which racial domination occupies a position entirely external to the logic of capital, and is 'not specific to the form of circulation and accumulation that constitutes the economic engine of capitalism'.[63] The corollary of this type of analysis is that movements for racial equality come to be seen as detracting from the class-based struggles necessary to confront capitalist power.[64] For Black Marxism, on the contrary, 'racial domination is constitutive of, rather than epiphenomenal to' the development of capitalism, or what some term 'racial capitalism'.[65]

Contra classical approaches of Marxism that give precedence to class as the main structuring relation of capitalism and at best 'add' other forms of oppression onto it, and culturalist or historical accounts that explain anti-blackness as part of the Western imagination, Black Marxism—associated early on with Cedric Robinson and related thinkers like Neville Alexander—conceptualises race as internal to the development of capitalism in ways that cannot simply be reduced to class.[66] Starting from the premise that class is not the only or main social relation in capitalist society, race is neither understood as a 'functional or derivative component of class rule', nor as sowing discord in an otherwise united working class or simply as the 'modality in which class is "lived"' and experienced.[67] Black Marxism thus bridges the 'faultline' between the 'politics of race' on the one hand and the 'politics of class' privileged by traditional Marxist approaches on the other.[68] Class is by no means the 'most fundamental dimension to capitalist society' and is instead a product of processes of valorisation.[69] The Black Marxist concept of 'racial capitalism' suggests that race is central to capitalism and cannot be reduced to class alone.[70] At the same time, in contrast to non-Marxist approaches to 'race', in the Black Marxist approach race is not a noun or ascribed attribute subject simply to 'voluntary acts of cultural determination' but is the product of 'ascriptive processes' structural to capitalist economic social life itself irrespective of the 'beliefs or intentions' of individual actors or interests.[71]

In particular, Black Marxism has applied this understanding of the relationship between race and class to the study of the role of slavery in the constitution of capitalist society. Specifically, Black Marxism points to how slavery has co-existed alongside wage labour within capitalism right up to the present day as part of a continuum of forced and unfree labour practices.[72] This displaces the relationship between capital and formally free wage labour as the 'privileged site of Marxist analysis', opening up the analysis to a broader range of moments and processes of exploitation and social domination better able to grasp 'the complex combination of both waged and un-waged labor that makes up the relations of production in modern capitalism'.[73] In a seminal article published nearly two decades ago, Bill Cooke bemoaned the incapacity of MOS to adequately theorise the antebellum plantation economy as part of the development of capitalism, rather than its precursor or aberration. He argued instead for the centrality of slavery to the development of contemporary industrial discipline.[74] Cooke shows that, in spite of the contentions of many historians, productivity-raising and valorisation processes were central in the scientific management of plantations, placing slavery fully within the political economy of capitalism. Marx himself had noted how the basis for the process of 'primitive accumulation' lay in 'New World plantation slavery, resource extraction, and the extermination of non-European populations on a world scale'.[75] He recognised that the precondition of cotton mills in the nascent capitalist industry was the production of cotton by slaves, pointing to the constitutive dialectical continuity between the unfree labour of New World slavery and the formally 'free' labour generally taken to characterise capitalist society.[76] In line with this understanding, Marx observed that antebellum slavery in the United States was not a mere vestige of a previous mode of production but was itself capitalist.

Extending these insights, the concept of 'racial capitalism' advanced by Black Marxism thus incorporates both slavery as a specifically racialised practice and 'extra-economic forms of coercion' into its understanding of not only the historical constitution but also the present reality of value, labour and capitalist accumulation. For Black Marxism, slavery is neither simply incidental to nor an echo resounding within the contemporary form assumed by antiblack racism, but a connection reproduced owing to 'contradictions alive in the present'.[77] Accordingly, its 'main import' consists in 'its ability to explain the persistence of racial domination within capitalist society without treating race as merely superstructural or irrelevant to regimes of capital accumulation'.[78] Whilst slavery appears in every chapter of *Capital*, Marx's account of primitive accumulation only features in its closing chapters, leaving much more to be said about the relationship between these processes and value as the principal form in which social relations are mediated in capitalist society.[79] Drawing from Aristotle, some in the Marxist tradition have taken the insight that as 'the secret of the expression of value', homogeneous labour depends upon 'formal freedom and equality' before the law, and is thus incompatible with conditions of slavery and forced labour.[80] This suggests that the value-form depends upon wage labour, leading to a 'tendency in both Marx and Marxists to sometimes identify capitalism with free wage labor'.[81] Against the tendency to identify capitalism with free wage labour, early Black Marxists posited the 'capitalist character of slavery', reinterpreting the struggles of slaves in America and the Caribbean as struggles against capitalism.[82]

Uniting Marx's CoPE with the theory and struggles of the Black radical tradition, a broader aim of Black Marxism is to play a role in developing a political capable of reconstituting a 'collective being' and 'ontological totality' that defies 'racial capitalist modes of differentiation' and the forms of value in which they are expressed.[83] Black Marxism's conceptualisation of racial capitalism thus holds important consequences for how value is understood. Capitalism is 'racial' in the sense that it accumulates through dispossession based on social difference, or 'the unequal differentiation of human value'.[84] Playing out in the accrual of 'uneven life chances' according to race, this is not solely expressed in 'slavery, colonialism, genocide, incarceration regimes, migrant exploitation, and contemporary racial warfare' but also, importantly, in less visibly and overtly violent practices that 'value and devalue forms of humanity differentially' in line with capitalist logics.[85] For Black Marxists like Robinson, Marx's method of abstraction elided the concrete reality of racial domination in the constitution of capitalist social forms like value.[86] As Frank Wilderson argues: 'we need a new language of abstraction to explain this horror'.[87]

For Sara-Maria Sorentino, however, Marx's abstractions are relevant to slavery insofar as slavery itself is 'an emergent abstraction of anti-blackness' that in fact represents the 'paradigmatic "real abstraction"' of the kind Marx associates with value, insofar as the 'abstract slave' is an expression of 'abstract labour' with a similarly 'real' existence.[88] The most sophisticated Marxian theories of value, by associating capitalist society with generalised and indirect abstract forms of domination rather than specific and direct relationships between capital and workers, keep open theoretical space to accommodate the persistence and reproduction of 'direct, overt forms of racial and gender domination' and the market-mediated management of populations subject to this domination.[89] According to Sorentino, 'both slavery and wage labour preceded capitalism, only to be rearticulated by it'.[90] In this perspective, slavery and wage labour are closely intertwined insofar as the 'freedom' of free wage labour is simultaneously unfree, wage labour and slave labour abstractly commensurate insofar as each is driven by the pursuit of expanded value in 'the whirlpool of an international market dominated by the capitalistic mode of production'.[91] From this perspective, there is nothing intrinsic to 'free labour' in the constitution of capitalism insofar as the 'self-expansion of value' that characterises capitalism is 'intrinsically indifferent to the [concrete] forms in which it dominates labour'.[92]

For these approaches inspired by the insights of Black Marxists, once the conceptualisation of capitalism is displaced from the 'freedom' of labour and towards a system of generalised dependence on markets for subsistence, slavery appears just as market-mediated as any other process of commodity production and consumption, slave labour bought and sold just as wage labour is.[93] In this sense, slave labour is different from that of the feudal serf prior to capitalism, because it is acquired with money and is destined to produce commodities. The buyer is incentivised to increase productivity as a means to realise surplus-value via the market.[94] At the same time, the 'free' character of wage labour has been constituted by its inverse in the 'unfree' character of slave labour, and with each associated a racialised identity, whiteness representing 'unslaveability and unalienable property' and Blackness its opposite. Racialised surplus populations have thus been continually included in capitalist accumulation precisely *through* their exclusion from wage labour. The management of these populations is determined and mediated by a generalised dependence on the market, just as capitalist abstractions 'absorbed the slave'.[95]

From the standpoint enabled by Black Marxist analyses, then, racial capitalism is associated with 'the despotism of the unwaged relation', insofar as the rights and forms of citizenship attached to waged work have been shaped by the exclusion of racialised populations from these rights and forms of citizenship.[96] But the Marxist focus on market mediation and the relationship of inclusion and exclusion with reference to wage labour does not tell the whole story here. A direct and violent relationship of terror against black bodies characterises antiblack racism independent of processes of economic exploitation and valuation. 'Fused with blackness', slavery and unfree labour appear as something more than a merely contingent economic relationship, acquiring the status of an 'ontological deficit, marked as an excessive violence outside politics or history'.[97] The theoretical tools afforded by Black Marxism expose how traditional Marxism has inadequately grasped 'white supremacy as the base' on which the economic and political relationships of the wage and civil society have been constructed, with the latter instead seeing racial domination representing 'an incidental part' of capitalism.[98] Capitalism, in this light, 'from its origins systematically . . . produc[es] and reproduce[es] "race" as global surplus humanity', dependent on the exploitation of unfree, unwaged labour.[99] The process of primitive accumulation does not cease with the establishment of capitalist social relations but is contained within every process of accumulation itself. Violence, then, is by no means excluded from a system of impersonal abstract social domination but 'situated immanently within it'.[100] Black Marxism here intersects with MOS scholarship informed by the concept of 'necrocapitalism', grounded in a 'state of exception' in which life is subjugated to death, and which highlights the persistence of a political economy based on violent 'dispossession and subjugation of life to the power of death'.[101] Black Marxism thus holds the potential to further open MOS to the study of the role of extra-economic coercion in mediating economic relations. Empirically, this might take the form of engagements with the relationship between racial domination, violence and the degree to which they are structurally reproduced by capitalist relations of production.

In a series of recent contributions, members of the Endnotes collective and others have used insights from Black Marxists to analyse the relationship between Black communities in the United States, police violence and the value-form. Drawing specifically upon the work of James Boggs, as well as Marx's conceptualisation of the 'surplus population' (or 'reserve

army of labour'), they relate the expulsion of Black workers from quality industrial jobs triggered by technological and economic change to the
subsequent policing of this 'surplus population' through an increasingly
carceral state.[102] After the initial integration of Black surplus populations as
slaves or wage labourers subject to a system of 'highly racialised wage dif-
ferentials' and labour conditions, the abolition of slavery and the subsequent
expulsion of labour from industry has created 'vast superfluous urban populations', resulting in an 'industrial reserve army' of the unemployed and
underemployed that is 'disproportionately non-white'. In the United States,
as industrial and technological change reshaped production and expelled
Black workers from quality dependable employment, their social status
was increasingly mediated not through the valorisation of labour power but
through the police and prison system as 'repressive, last-resort social mediation'.[103] When labour markets tightened in the post-war years, competition
for jobs decreased and with it the pressures to allocate employment according to racialised social divisions. This dynamic afforded political space for
the civil rights movement to advance demands for legal equality, which
resulted in equal opportunities and affirmative action legislation.

With falling profit rates in the 1970s, however, demand for labour plum-
meted. The end of legal segregation created a new reserve army, a surplus
population to be managed through the 'rise of the US carceral state'. Released
from regulation of social relations by means of the labour market and confined to urban locales newly deprived of private and public investment and
infrastructure, the fraying social fabric of Black communities in the United
States was increasingly socially mediated by police force, a trend which
continues to this day.[104] In response to the 'end of secure wage labour and
the withdrawal of public welfare provisions', the state mediated 'wageless
life' through policing 'unproductive' populations with a peripheral relationship to the production of value.[105] As Sylvia Winter writes, in soaking up
these surplus populations, 'the ghettos and prisons of today's North America
are the new forms of the plantation archipelago'.[106] Punishment here acts as
a 'medium for equalization' in the absence of employment, incarceration as
a means to maintain the abstract social mediation of human activity without
the expenditure of concrete labour. Abstract domination proceeds here not
through abstract labour time but, as with the abstract slave before, what
Sorentino calls the 'abstract criminal'. This reveals what has long been the
case, but that Marxism has and still struggles to grasp: whilst power in capitalist society often operates through formally impersonal processes, force
itself 'participates in labor's abstraction into the value-form'.[107] In this way,
racial capitalism relates not only to the differential 'assignment of relative
economic value' to human lives but also to their 'differential vulnerability

to state violence' as part and parcel of the organisation and management of capitalist social relations.[108]

In such analyses, Black Marxism highlights the continuing relevance of the Marxian concept of value to comprehending key contemporary challenges. As a theoretical frame, it invites and illuminates the empirical study of how specific processes of social mediation connect domination and antagonism across a wide institutional and everyday terrain where lines blur between capital and the state. This has important consequences for empirical research agendas focused on surplus populations paradoxically included in processes of capitalist valorisation precisely through their exclusion, for whom difference operates as a ground of domination. The informal and precarious position in which such populations are placed is mediated not only by the employment relationship but also by the power of the state to legislate, police and incarcerate. Black Marxism thus clearly points to the limits of Marxian organisational analysis solely focusing on struggles of formally free workers in the labour market, the firm and the labour process. Black Marxism broadens the horizon of Marxian analysis to address what is commonly excluded and which is nonetheless essential to the reproduction of capitalism: an outside demarcated by racial difference and enforced through the potential for state violence.

On the critique of antiblackness and the critique of antisemitism

The analysis of antiblackness is only one way in which MOS can confront contemporary racism in contemporary capitalism. In the aftermath of the 2008 financial crisis, on left and right alike a popular and populist imaginary arose which related the threat of outside forces to the national community of productive, hardworking people. This included, at various times and in various places, and to varying political ends, a cast of characters incorporating welfare recipients, migrants, bankers and international financial institutions. This was given new teeth by the blossoming of right-wing populism in Brexit and Trumpism, but the left did not remain immune from the appeal of this politics. At the same time, social media and the spread of the world wide web has mainlined, and in some cases mainstreamed, conspiracy theories into the worldviews of voters, workers, activists and everyday life. These conspiracy theories often seek to personalise ultimately impersonal and abstract forms of financial and economic power as resting in the hands of scheming, shadowy elites or minorities. This provided an online environment for the real-world spread of new forms of racism that responded to global conflicts and crises, as well as an increase in established, persistent forms of racism—in particular antisemitism, as a very specific kind of racism.[109]

Particularly of relevance to the theories and concepts discussed in this book is the role critical Marxism has taken in confronting antisemitism. As antisemitism has taken on new dimensions in the past decades, critical Marxist approaches have been used to understand it as a specific form of racism that often adopts a superficially anti-capitalist or anti-elite posture tied, implicitly or explicitly, to questions of work and economic life. The lineage of the CoPE that runs through the Frankfurt School critical theory of Adorno and Horkheimer, through the value critique of Moishe Postone and the open Marxism of Werner Bonefeld has strongly emphasised the historical and contemporary importance of antisemitism in modern capitalist society and its connection with key categories of labour, money, value and abstraction.[110] In particular, antisemitism has been conceptualised as arising from a foreshortened or truncated critique of capitalism that concretises and personalises in the figure of the Jew (or, through displacement, the state of Israel) responsibility for the abstract forms and structural effects that characterise capitalist society. This connects antisemitism as a specific kind of racism with a deficient politics of work and production that spans both right and left of the political spectrum.

The critical objective to decode and confront antisemitism was important to the Frankfurt School. Seeing antisemitism as intrinsic to Nazism, Adorno's categorical imperative was that the world should never again create the conditions by which the Holocaust could be allowed to happen: 'Hitler has imposed a new categorical imperative upon humanity in the state of their unfreedom: to arrange their thinking and conduct, so that Auschwitz never repeats itself, so that nothing similar ever happen again'.[111] The implication of such an imperative is that theorists in this tradition hold to a CoPE doggedly resistant to conspiracy theory, authoritarianism, totalitarianism and nationalism. In particular, this strand of critical theory has analysed how antisemitism does not simply 'articulate anti-capitalism in a displaced manner', misguidedly focusing on the wrong target, but rather 'criticizes capitalism as a system of Jewish power' itself. This truncated critique of capitalism has typically centred on two elements: first, the condemnation of financial capitalism as a world-market reality of effortless wealth; and, second, the endorsement of productive capital as a material force and foundation of national wealth.[112]

In the famous 'Elements of Antisemitism' section of their *Dialectic of Enlightenment*, Adorno and Horkheimer comment that contemporary antisemitism arose initially from a class shift from the rule of aristocrats who resented work to that of industrialists who championed their own productiveness.[113] The latter became synonymous with production in a shared enterprise with workers. Industry was seen as the productive force in society, and, with the development of capitalism over this period, the class antagonism in production was further elided in formal legal equivalence between the buyers and sellers of labour power. This bore consequences for how the activities of circulation were understood, the antagonism concealed in production ideologically transplanted to the buying of goods with the wage. Exploitation, whilst unclear in the workplace, became apparent to workers in a distorted fashion according to how far the wage went to meet the price asked for goods. As such, groups who hold a popular association with the activities of circulation owing to their historical exclusion from established professions—such as Jews, who in many societies had until relatively recently found themselves confined to less established forms of activity like shopkeeping, merchant services and so on—bore the brunt of a distorted confrontation with the class antagonism.[114] This came to be filtered through an antisemitic critique of nascent capitalism that posed what is apparently productive—the national community of workers and industrialists—against that which is apparently not—the activities of the circulation and consumption of goods and services, and those responsible for them.

For contemporary scholars in this theoretical lineage, present-day critiques of class society by means of a critique of unproductive sections of the population—such as financiers, bankers or the 'elite'—carry this same background, calling into service appeals to the 'national community of hardworking people' affronted by a parasitical external force. This way, conspiracy theory critiques personifications of economic categories. But '[t]he critique of the banker . . . misses the object of critique', which should be the real abstraction itself—whether value, money, capital—and not its bearer.[115] Personalising anonymous, incomprehensible powers in a series of scheming figures, ranging from financiers to the state of Israel, these conspiracy theories conform to the worst tendencies of what Adorno and Horkheimer call 'ticket-thinking', the acritical practice of 'attach[ing] labels to social things without further thought as to what these things might be'—stopping short at identifying immediate and concrete culprits for the socially mediated and abstract forms, such as value and money, in which capitalist social relations appear.[116]

Connecting this Frankfurt School inheritance with ideas from Black Marxism, Hylton White expands this analysis of the relationship between fetish forms and antisemitism to address antiblack racism and antisemitism together through the prism of their relationship with work, labour and value.[117] Drawing from the work of Moishe Postone and Frantz Fanon, White locates antiblackness in the racist association of blackness with 'a feral bodily power that can be socialised only by taming it', a 'brute biological force that lacks self-governing will and is thus in need of socialising violence to make it useful to civil society'. Simultaneously presented as both 'potent' and 'recalcitrant', antiblack racism suggests that the 'essentially biological body' ascribed to blackness can be utilised as a 'force of production' only when 'harnessed with dominating power' by capital or the state. In this, just as antisemitism personifies real abstraction in the figure of the Jew, antiblack racism personifies in the black body abstract labour as a 'social force abstracted from individual or wilful action', a 'visceral human capacity'.[118] This personification is the dialectical mirror image, White suggests, of how, owing to a precapitalist legacy of anti-Jewish racism centring on 'the identification of Jews with commerce and usury', antisemites personify in the figure of the Jew abstract wealth or 'dematerialised value'. White argues that 'the ideological pair of antisemitism and antiblack racism gives us human proxies for these fetish forms'—abstract labour and abstract value—'casting the pathologies of modernity not as the outcome of a structure of alienation, but as the powers of antisocial racial types'.[119] Where these diverge is insofar as the abstract monetary valorisation antisemites personify in the figure of the Jew represents 'a power of control' whereas the abstract biological capacity antiblack racists personify in the black body represents 'a power that requires control'.

This plays out in the everyday lived existence that these racisms take in society. Fanon notes how, where antisemitism associates Jewishness with the intellectual and abstract wealth and power wielded by a whole race, seeking the persecution of all Jews on this totalising basis, antiblack racism seeks the domination of embodied Black subjects in the context of their immediate and concrete 'corporeality'.[120] On this reading, antisemitism represents the 'paranoid fear of a people engaged in conspiracies of will' orchestrated by an 'invisible, untraceable intelligence', inviting its adherents to pursue a totalising violence that aims to 'flush out and destroy an entire people, as a people'. Antiblackness, meanwhile, associates blackness not with control and thus the destruction of a whole race but rather with 'an uncontrolled bodily energy' to be dominated in its specifically 'concrete, corporeal, visible' instantiations. For Fanon, 'this is the key generic difference between the industrialised mass murder of the Holocaust and the ritualised destruction of the individual black body by a lynching mob'. In both cases, abstract social forms, whether labour or value, are personalised in human concrete forms by racists, with these concrete forms then to be either dominated or destroyed. Antisemitism and antiblackness also coincide in that each carries its own 'dangerously misleading form of emancipatory fantasy'. Antisemitism promises its adherents resistance against a 'fetishistic representation of capital', something that motivates some specifically 'left-wing' forms of antisemitism. Antiblackness, meanwhile, promises its proponents a disastrously misplaced resistance against abstract labour as an expression of human unfreedom under capitalism, White suggests, motivating far-right movements in particular.

Just as antisemitism personifies in Jewishness the abstract character of monetary power in capitalist society, antiblackness thus also expresses, in a distorted and dangerous fashion, 'an opposition generated repeatedly within the forms of capitalist society', as White writes, human practice appearing in the perverted form of 'fetishistic representations of its own functioning' sourced from the wellspring of existing prejudices. Capitalist categories like value and labour are read through the lens of a racist worldview because 'the valorisation of capital is the outcome of an extraordinarily complex social process, and that complex social process unfolds in a way that obscures its social conditions', not solely because of the illusions of social actors but as a matter of the appearances being necessary to the conditions of reproduction of the process itself.[121] Together, Black Marxism and the critique of antisemitism show that critical approaches to work and economic life in capitalist society, and thus of management and organisation more broadly, can contribute vital tools to grasp the social conditions obscured behind the fetish forms of a society ruled by the abstract force of value, and thus practically contribute towards the fight against antiblack racism—and, moreover, antisemitism.

Ecological Marxism: nature and social metabolism

As contemporary movements for civil rights and racial equality have drawn attention to the deep links between racism and capitalist political economy over recent years, a range of other mobilisations and movements have drawn attention to the climate crisis as one of the main existential threats facing humankind at the present time and into the future. This has had a parallel impact in Marxism, focusing the minds of Marxist theorists on the relationship between capitalism and the environment. Represented in the work of John Bellamy Foster, Paul Burkett and others, ecological Marxism theorises the relationship between humankind and nature by positing that, materially estranged from the 'natural conditions of their existence', humans dominate and objectify these conditions in order to live.[122] However, under capitalism, the transformation of nature to serve human needs and purposes simultaneously erodes and degrades these conditions. The capitalist production and valorisation process is a historically specific mediation of the intrinsic 'separation' of humankind from nature.[123] As in any other mode of production, humans realise their subjectivity through its objectification in the transformation of natural resources into useful or exchangeable things. Accordingly, what distinguishes 'the worst of architects from the best of bees' is a separateness of humankind from nature encapsulated in the capacity of the former to conceive of designs and enact them in products in which both external nature is transformed into something useful or desirable and humans themselves become subjects.[124]

Humanity's transformation of nature however occurs under social and historical conditions not of its choosing.[125] The social metabolism under capitalism represents the current 'particular, alienated form' the metabolic relationship between humans and nature assumes in practice.[126] The metabolism between humans and nature, then, is the basic process through which capitalism socially mediates the relation between humans and nature, organising and constituting 'the basis on which life is sustained and growth and reproduction becomes possible'.[127] The social metabolism relates not only to the 'actual metabolic interaction between nature and society through human labour', but also more broadly to 'the complex, dynamic, interdependent set of needs and relations brought into being and constantly reproduced in alienated form under capitalism'.[128] The concept captures not a static or essentialist notion of nature and society but a 'highly dynamic relationship reflecting changes in the ways human beings mediate between nature and society through production'.[129]

The understanding of metabolism underpins a theorisation of environmental crisis based upon the notion of a 'metabolic rift', or 'an irreparable rift in the interdependent process of the social metabolism'.[130] The metabolic rift refers to the degradation of both nature and the human in their 'metabolic interaction'.[131] The literature on metabolic rift suggests that contemporary conditions have exacerbated the environmental degradation in which it results, including the degradation of labour power, which constitutes the mode of existence of humans under capital, or, as Marx writes, 'the material of nature transposed into a human organism'.[132] Nonetheless, this contradiction is not exceptional but rather *constitutive* of capitalism, reflecting its basic crisis tendency due to the overproduction of goods relative to the capacity of workers to consume them.[133] This tendency centres on the contradiction between the conditions of production and the conditions of consumption, in which each places constraints on the other. Goods must be sold, but the 'capital–labour antagonism' implies that workers face limits in the value of the goods they can consume through the wage to reproduce their labour power.

Meanwhile, the 'capital-ecology antagonism' erodes and degrades the conditions of production and reproduction, limiting accumulation and disrupting the 'realization of surplus value'.[134] This contradiction is expressed just as much in 'defunding public education or the deterioration of vital infrastructures' as it is in 'soil exhaustion or deforestation'. In all cases, capitalism exhausts that on which it relies—'human labour power, built environments and resources'—increasing barriers to accumulation and reproduction but with no promise of terminal collapse or resolution. The global economy must constantly work against the underlying tendency to crises of overproduction, symptomatic of a system so rapacious as to risk environmental ruin. The metabolic rift thus represents a permanent, if dynamic, state of affairs logically and historically hardwired into capitalism's contradictory and conflict-ridden functioning.

Alongside a dedicated journal, *Organization & Environment*, at the time of writing the conceptualisation of metabolism and metabolic rift has to date been taken up a handful of times elsewhere in critical MOS.[135] However, this uptake has not been explicitly linked to value, on which ecological Marxists place increasing emphasis.[136] Their understanding centres on the relationship between use-value and exchange-value. On the one hand, use-value and the concrete labour associated with it is understood as a 'natural form' linked to the human intercourse with nature. On the other, exchange value and the abstract labour associated with it represent the alienation of use-value, and, through ongoing processes of primitive accumulation, the externalisation and exploitation of nature. Capitalist accumulation implies an inherent tendency of capitalism towards ecological destruction.

One particularly provocative application of the theory of metabolic rift to the topic of value is Ariel Salleh's conceptualisation of the 'metabolic value' produced by work as a social metabolism with nature.[137] Salleh uses this term to draw attention to the role of 'workers, nominally outside of capitalism [i.e. not in waged work producing commodities for exchange on the market], whose labor catalyzes metabolic transformations' and mediates the metabolic rift.[138] This gendered and racialised 'meta-industrial labour' spans 'indigenous cultivators in the Global South' and workers in the 'non-monetized domestic sphere' of the Global North, centring in all contexts on the interchange with nature in the form of the provisioning of food and shelter and the reproduction of bodies and labour power. The 'metabolic value' produced in these forms of interchange with nature, Salleh suggests, is a category of struggle against and beyond capitalist value that takes account not only of nature but also of the unpaid and unrecognised 'regenerative' labour that bridges and mediates humanity's exploitative and alienated relationship with it. Taken up in critically oriented MOS, Salleh's conceptualisation of the metabolic value produced by these subjects in mediating the metabolic rift has been usefully combined with the insights of the SRT discussed earlier.[139]

Ecological Marxist concepts of metabolic rift and metabolic value have helped shed light upon empirical case studies of the so-called 'circular economy', and in particular what has been termed 'circular economy from below' rooted in everyday practices of paid and unpaid work and 'green-collar' labour.[140] The term 'circular economy' captures a variety of approaches centring on the rerouting of waste into the production of goods and ultimately value. There are divergent applications of circular economy principles in production, from 'whole-system' approaches that strike directly at the heart of the metabolism between humans and nature by redesigning 'socio-ecological relations' in a more 'regenerative and redistributive' direction, to more granular approaches dealing in local food practices and urban ecologies accounted for in the case studies collected in a recent special issue of *Culture & Organization*.[141]

Corporate applications of 'circular economy from above' preserve the current metabolic configuration of production and consumption, depoliticising waste by presenting it as a mere operational inefficiency that can be recouped as part of a more sustainable version of how goods are produced. For instance, at companies like Apple, planned obsolescence goes hand-in-hand with circular economy credentials, legitimising the turnover of technological goods and valorising the e-waste in which they result.[142] Zero-waste is promoted in these mainstream applications as an operational organising principle that ensures 'ever-replenishing growth without any residues'. But critical empirical work on the application of zero-waste as an operating principle argues that, as a condition of this growth, capitalism's inevitable production of waste is an 'inherent by-product' of 'the excessive exploitation of labour and the environment'. In this respect, waste is 'wasted labour . . . equal to the rotten and valueless of the world: those who embody the traumatic failure of megalopolitan capitalism'.[143] There is thus a 'materiality' and an 'embodiment' concealed in how circular economy practices revalorise waste as valuable. The mainstream narrative of the circular economy as a convenient optimisation of production and valorisation elides the contradictory and antagonistic context of the metabolic rift, and overlooks the everyday unpaid work and waged labour that the circular economy requires.[144] Apple, specifically, has portrayed its e-waste management, disposal and recycling as being conducted cleanly and seamlessly by robots. This conceals the actual and arduous conditions of life and labour in the largely informal work that physically metabolises obsolescent technology into reusable waste in the Global South and elsewhere, and valorises the waste itself, rather than the labour that transforms it, as something with its own economic value.[145]

The ecological Marxist understanding of the social metabolism would rather highlight the role not only of dedicated 'green' jobs but also of the 'meta-industrial labour' that helps constitute circularity in production and circulation processes.[146] Central to the metabolic transformation of nature, this labour largely rests in unpaid spheres of provisioning and social reproduction, 'from below'. In the Global South, for instance, waste is processed through a material and embodied relationship with the work and labour of 'millions of people [who] have been wasted socially (i.e. segregated, impoverished, abused) and forcefully displaced to environments where rubbish accumulates and livelihoods are threatened if not totally contaminated'.[147] Meanwhile, in the Global North, waste management is increasingly associated with the responsibilisation of individuals in the domestic sphere of social reproduction, centring on everyday actions of recycling, repairing and restoring. These everyday forms of circularity ascribe 'metabolic value' to waste by mediating and remediating the metabolic rift.

Recognising this interrelationship between 'political narratives of waste management' such as the circular economy and the 'embodied experience' of concrete subjects can help the identification of strategies to 'unplug' the 'circular political economy' from the corporate and intervene politically in the social metabolism it mediates.[148] In this 'circular economy from below', for instance, we can locate forms of grassroots experimentation like repair cafes and food waste saving schemes that open out upon the prospect of radical alternatives that re-mediate the social metabolism in new ways. These practices represent a modality of struggle over the metabolic valorisation of waste and the forms and purposes it serves—or what has been termed 'circular economy for social revolution'.[149]

An ecological Marxist rereading of the circular economy thereby suggests a research agenda that reconnects the politics of consumption and a more explicitly antagonistic politics of production. Recognising that any confrontation with value implies a focus on both, research would explore how what one consumes and how one acquires it relates to the conditions and compulsions under which one produces, as two sides of the social-ecological metabolism of humans with nature. In doing so, it would bring labour struggles and (classed, gendered or racialised) subjectivities into the study of environmental crisis and the top-down policy proposals and bottom-up social movements that have formed in response to it. Ultimately, to address the climate crisis, MOS needs to address capitalism itself.

***

The new directions in Marxian MOS we have mapped and introduced here contribute towards the contestation of the forms through which labour and human life are mediated in capitalist society, and help shed light on the possible alternatives that could arise within and beyond them. Each of the new directions deploys a Marxian understanding to go beyond the limited appraisal within traditional Marxist conceptualisation of class, gender, race and the ecology. Addressing the question of value as the dominant social form that mediates all social relations, the Marxist strands presented in this chapter expand Marxist MOS by unveiling and including constitutive elements within capitalism as a totality—social reproductive work, nature, unfree labour, etc.—traditionally left theoretically uninterrogated and empirically unexamined. These elements are not understood as existing externally to capitalism and superimposed onto it, but rather as essential to its existence. These theories de-centre the understanding of work, including a variety of forms of work, such as unpaid and unfree work, next to commodified labour power, which has traditionally been at the core of Marxian analyses. These multiple forms of work are both predicated on capitalism and essential to its reproduction: without socially reproductive work, no labour force is available to sell its labour power; without the policing and incarceration of surplus populations, no reserve army of labour can be maintained; and without the often informalised work of waste management in the Global South, any 'circular' alternative to carbon capitalism cannot be sustained. The analysis of these phenomena can inform, we argue, new understandings of work, value and class, which are necessary to theorise the heterogeneous antagonistic struggles characterising contemporary capitalism. This opens up the analysis of class to include subjectivities produced at the interface between waged work and the socially reproductive sphere, in highly fragmented labour markets including non-waged labour, and in patterns of capitalist development across the Global South and the Global North predicated on ongoing primitive accumulation. These gendered, racialised and geographically inscribed subjectivities are not incidental to processes of capitalist valorisation, but rather constitutive of it.

Traditionally taken to refer to a process that *precedes* capitalism, among the alternative approaches to primitive accumulation advocated here, each recognises the continuing historical salience of Marx's observation that

> the discovery of gold and silver in America, the extirpation, enslavement and entombment in mines of the indigenous population of that continent, the beginnings of the conquest and plunder of India, the conversion of Africa into a preserve for the commercial hunting of black-skins, are all things which characterise *the dawn* of the era of capitalist production.[150]

The new directions presented in this chapter, whether focused on social reproduction, race or ecological destruction, coalesce around such an appraisal of the ongoing character of this process of primitive accumulation in coexistence with capitalist social relations, rather than their historically distinct precondition. In doing so, these new directions go further than Marxism has traditionally in relating processes of primitive accumulation with empirical issues like the reshaping of the domestic sphere, the creation and enslavement of racialised surplus populations, or the plunder of the earth's natural resources. These streams of Marxism enable us to expand Marxist MOS research in ways that are consonant with other strands of MOS that have paid increasing attention to some of these processes of dispossession and primitive accumulation.[151] However, existing work tends to proceed from a perspective that makes less of a connection with Marxist categories like value. The connection of the sociality of value and other economic categories with the materiality of processes of primitive accumulation, dispossession, ecological exhaustion and social reproduction thus represents a potential new direction for Marxist MOS and MOS more broadly.

Notes

1 View all titles in the *Open Marxism* series at Pluto Press: www.plutobooks. com/pluto-series/open-marxism/
2 Bonefeld W (2014) *Critical Theory and the Critique of Political Economy*. London: Bloomsbury; Bonefeld W (2016a) Negative dialectics and critique of economic objectivity. *History of the Human Sciences* 29(2): 60–76; Bonefeld W (2016b) Bringing critical theory back in at a time of misery. *Capital & Class* 40(2): 233–244; Clarke S (1991) State, class struggle and the reproduction of capital. In: Clarke S (ed.) *The State Debate*. Basingstoke: Macmillan; Dinerstein AC (2015) *The Politics of Autonomy in Latin America*. Basingstoke: Palgrave; Gunn R (1987a) Marxism and mediation. *Common Sense* 2: 57–66; Gunn R (1987b) Notes on class. *Common Sense* 2: 15–25; Gunn R (1992) Against historical materialism: Marxism as first-order discourse. In: Bonefeld W, Gunn R, Psychopedis K (eds.) *Open Marxism II*. London: Pluto, pp. 1–45; Holloway J (2010) *Crack Capitalism*. London: Pluto.
3 Charnock G (2010) Challenging new state spatialities. *Antipode* 42: 1279–1303 (1284).
4 Adorno TW (1990) *Negative Dialectics*. London: Routledge.
5 Gunn 1992.
6 Bonefeld 2014: 102.
7 Gunn 1987b.
8 Bonefeld 2016b: 238.
9 Bonefeld 2014: 43.
10 Bonefeld 2014: 107.
11 Bonefeld W (2016c) Science, hegemony and action. *Journal of Social Sciences* 12(2): 19–41 (34).
12 Bonefeld 2016b: 241; Marcuse H (1972) *One Dimensional Man*. London: Abacus, 90.
13 Bonefeld 2014.
14 Bonefeld 2016a.
15 Gunn 1987a, 1992.
16 Gunn 1987a: 57–58.
17 Bonefeld W (1994) Human practice and perversion. *Common Sense* 15: 43–52.
18 Clarke 1991: 185; Gunn 1987b: 60.

19 Clarke S (1992) The global accumulation of capital and the periodisation of the capitalist state form. In: Bonefeld W, Gunn R, Psychopedis K (eds.) *Open Marxism I: Dialectics and History*. London: Pluto, pp. 133–179 (136).
20 Gunn 1992, 1987b: 63; Marx K (1976) *Capital*. Vol. 1. London: Penguin, 198.
21 Bonefeld 2014: 175; Bonefeld 1987: 68.
22 Gunn 1992: 32.
23 Dinerstein 2015: 21–22.
24 Holloway 2010.
25 Bonefeld 2014: 224–226.
26 Gunn 1987b: 64.
27 Adorno TW (2003a) Reflections on class theory. In: Tiedemann R (ed.) *Can One Live after Auschwitz?* Stanford: Stanford University Press, pp. 93–110 (122).
28 Bonefeld 2014: 213.
29 Adorno TW (2003b) Late capitalism or industrial society? In: Tiedemann R (ed.) *Can One Live After Auschwitz?* Stanford: Stanford University Press, pp. 111–125 (104).
30 Adorno 2003b: 105.
31 Dinerstein AC (2010) Autonomy in Latin America: Between resistance and integration. *Community Development Journal* 45(3): 356–366 (357–358, 360–361, 364).
32 Neary M, Taylor G (1998) *Money and the Human Condition*. London: Macmillan, 107.
33 Neary & Taylor 1998: 123.
34 Neary & Taylor 1998.
35 Dinerstein 2010: 357–358, 364.
36 Dinerstein 2015.
37 Holloway 2010.
38 Bhattacharya T (2017a) Introduction: Mapping social reproduction theory. In: Bhatthacharya T (ed.) *Social Reproduction Theory*. London: Pluto Press, pp. 1–20; Bhattacharya T (2017b) How not to skip class. In: Bhatthacharya T (ed.) *Social Reproduction Theory*. London: Pluto Press, pp. 68–93; Dalla Costa M, James S (1972) *Women and the Subversion of the Community*. Bristol: Falling Wall Press; Federici S (2012) *Revolution at Point Zero*. Oakland: PM Press; Vogel L (1983/2013) *Marxism and the Oppression of Women*. Chicago: Haymarket.
39 Bezanson K, Luxton M (eds.) (2006) *Social Reproduction*. Montreal: McGill's-Queen's University Press, 3.
40 Luxton M (2006) Feminist political economy in Canada and the politics of social reproduction. In: Bezanson K, Luxton M (eds.) *Social Reproduction*. Montreal: McGill's-Queen's University Press, p. 24.
41 Ferguson S, McNally D (2015) Social reproduction beyond intersectionality. *Viewpoint Magazine*, 5. Available at: https://viewpointmag.com/2015/10/31/social-reproduction-beyond-intersectionality-an-interview-with-sue-ferguson-and-david-mcnally/
42 Dalla Costa M (1995) Capitalism and reproduction. In: Bonefeld W, Gunn R, Holloway J, Psychopedis K (eds.) *Open Marxism III*. London: Pluto, pp. 7–16; Denning, M. (2010) Wageless life. *New Left Review*, 66: 79–97 (80); Marx 1976: 723.
43 Marx 1976: 274.

44 Bezanson K (2006) The neo-liberal state and social reproduction. In: Bezanson K, Luxton M (eds.) *Social Reproduction*. Montreal: McGill's-Queen's University Press, pp. 173–214 (175).
45 Yeates N (2012) Global care chains. *Global Networks* 12(2): 135–154.
46 Luxton 2006; Vogel 1983/2013.
47 Dalla Costa & James 1972; Federici 2012.
48 Fraser N (2016) Contradictions of capital and care. *New Left Review* 100: 99–117; Fraser N (2017) Crisis of care? In: Bhattacharya T (ed.) *Social Reproduction Theory*. London: Pluto, pp. 21–36.
49 Bhattacharya 2017a; Vogel 1983/2013.
50 Hartmann H (1979) The unhappy marriage of Marxism and feminism. *Capital & Class* 8: 1–33; Molyneux M (1979) Beyond the domestic labour debate. *New Left Review* 116: 3–27; Young I (1981) Beyond the unhappy marriage. In: Sargent L (ed.) *Women and Revolution*. Boston: South End Press, pp. 43–69.
51 Dalla Costa & James 1972.
52 Bhattacharya 2017a; Federici 2012.
53 Federici 2012: 8.
54 Fraser 2016; Fraser 2017; Ferguson S (2017) Children, childhood and capitalism. In: Bhattacharya T (ed.) *Social Reproduction Theory*. London: Pluto, pp. 68–93.
55 Dalla Costa & James 1972; Federici 2012.
56 Hopkins CT (2017) Mostly work, little pay. In: Bhattacharya T (ed.) *Social Reproduction Theory*. London: Pluto, pp. 131–147.
57 Federici 2012.
58 Ruiz Castro M, Grau-Grau M, Lupu I, Daskalaki M, McGinn K (2019) Social reproduction: Intra-household relations, organizational initiatives and public policies. Call for papers for a special issue of *Gender, Work & Organization*; Miszczynski M (2019) Mutual dependency: Offshored labour and family organisation in post-socialist Romania. *Organization*. doi:10.1177/1350508419838690; Zanoni, 2019. As work was being completed on this chapter, COVID-19 appeared to have sparked new interest in SRT, including an excellent article forthcoming (at the time of writing) in *Organization* relating concepts of social reproduction to the pandemic—see Mezzadri A (forthcoming) Social reproduction and pandemic neoliberalism. *Organization*.
59 Zanoni 2019.
60 Felstiner A (2011) Working the crowd: Employment and labor law in the crowdsourcing industry. *Berkeley Journal of Employment and Labor Law* 32(1): 143–203 (152).
61 Bhattacharya 2017a.
62 Miszczyński 2019.
63 Chen C (2013) The limit point of capitalist equality. *Endnotes* 3: 202–223; Harvey D (2015) *Seventeen Contradictions and the End of Capitalism*. New York: Oxford University Press, 7–8; Issar S (2020) Listening to black lives matter. *Contemporary Political Theory*. doi:10.1057/s41296-020-00399-0. In places, this section draws upon Pitts FH (2020) *Value*. Cambridge: Polity.
64 Harvey D (2007) *A Brief History of Neoliberalism*. New York: Oxford University Press, 41–43; Roediger D (2017) *Race, Class and Marxism*. London: Verso.
65 Issar 2020: 10.

66 Robinson C (1983/2000) *Black Marxism*. University of North Carolina Press; Alexander N (1979) *One Azania, One Nation*. London: Zed; White H (2020) How is capitalism racial? Fanon, critical theory and the fetish of antiblackness. *Social Dynamics* 46(1): 22–35.
67 Hall, quoted in Chen 2013; Alexander 1979; White 2020.
68 Chen 2013.
69 White 2020.
70 Robinson 1983/2000.
71 Chen 2013.
72 Banaji J (2003) The fictions of free labour. *Historical Materialism* 11(3): 69–95; Issar 2020; Robinson 1983/2000.
73 Lowe 2015, cited in Issar 2020: 12.
74 Cooke B (2003) The denial of slavery in management studies. *Journal of Management Studies* 40(8): 1895–1918 (1901).
75 Chen 2013.
76 Clegg J (2020) A theory of capitalist slavery. *Journal of Historical Sociology* 33(1): 74–98 (75).
77 White 2020: 11–12.
78 Issar 2020: 12–13.
79 Sorentino SM (2019a) The abstract slave. *International Labor and Working-Class History* 96: 17–37.
80 Sorentino SM (2019b) Natural slavery, real abstraction, and the virtuality of anti-blackness. *Theory & Event* 22(3): 630–673 (631).
81 Clegg 2020: 76; Patterson O (1977) Slavery. *Annual Review of Sociology* 3: 407–449.
82 James CLR (1938/2001) *Black Jacobins*. London: Penguin; DuBois W (1935/1999) *Black Reconstruction*. New York: Free Press; Clegg 2020: 76.
83 Melamed J (2015) Racial capitalism. *Critical Ethnic Studies* 1(1): 76–85 (79–80); Robinson 1983/2000.
84 Melamed 2015: 77.
85 Melamed 2015: 77.
86 Robinson 1983/2000; Sorentino 2019a: 18.
87 Cited in Sorentino 2019a: 20.
88 Sorentino 2019a: 18; Sorentino 2019b: 632.
89 Chen 2013.
90 Sorentino 2019a: 20–25.
91 Marx, quoted in Sorentino 2019a: 21.
92 Banaji, quoted in Sorentino 2019a: 22.
93 Clegg JJ (2015) Capitalism and slavery. *Critical Historical Studies* 2(2): 281–304 (301).
94 Clegg 2015; Cooke 2003.
95 Chen 2013; Sorentino 2019a: 27.
96 Wilderson F (2003) Gramsci's Black Marx. *Social Identities* 9(2): 225–240 (230).
97 Sorentino 2019b: 631–632.
98 Wilderson 2003: 225; Chen 2013.
99 Chen 2013.
100 Sorentino 2019: 23.
101 Banerjee SB (2008) Necrocapitalism. *Organization Studies* 29(12): 1541–1563 (1541).

102 Boggs J (2009/1963) *The American Revolution.* New York: Monthly Review; Johnson C (2011) James Boggs, the 'Outsiders,' and the challenge of postindustrial society. *Souls* 13(3): 303–326; Clegg JJ, Lucas R (2015) Brown v. Ferguson. *Endnotes* 4: 10–69 (63–66).

103 Chen 2013.

104 Clegg & Lucas 2015.

105 Denning 2010: 79–97; Chen 2013.

106 Unpublished manuscript *Metamorphosis* quoted in Sorentino 2019: 31.

107 Sorentino 2019: 31–32.

108 Chen 2013.

109 Bolton M, Pitts FH (2018) *Corbynism: A Critical Approach.* Bingley: Emerald.

110 Adorno TW, Horkheimer M (1972) *The Dialectic of Enlightenment.* London: Verso; Postone M (2006) History and helplessness. *Public Culture* 18(1): 93–110; Bonefeld 2014.

111 Adorno TW (2003) In: Tiedemann R (ed.) *Can One Live After Auschwitz?* Stanford: Stanford University Press, p. 358.

112 Bonefeld 2014: 205.

113 Adorno & Horkheimer 1972: 173–174.

114 Aufheben (2017) The rise of conspiracy theories. *Aufheben* #24: 12–28.

115 Bonefeld 2016b: 237.

116 Adorno & Horkheimer 1972: 205; Bonefeld 2014: 203.

117 White 2020; Postone M (2003) The holocaust and the trajectory of the twentieth century. In: Postone M, Santner E (eds.) *Catastrophe and Meaning.* Chicago: University of Chicago Press, pp. 81–114; Fanon F (1986) *Black Skins, White Masks.* London: Pluto. The three paragraphs that follow draw from Pitts 2020: 49–51.

118 White 2020: 10.

119 White 2020: 2–3.

120 Fanon 1986: 125–127.

121 White 2020: 2, 9, 11–12.

122 Foster JB (1999) Marx's theory of metabolic rift. *American Journal of Sociology* 105(2): 366–405 (383); Burkett P (1996) Value, capital and nature. *Science & Society* 60(3): 332–359.

123 Marx K (1973) *Grundrisse.* London: Penguin, 489; Foster JB (2016) Marxism in the anthropocene. *International Critical Thought* 6(3): 393–421 (403).

124 Marx 1976: 284–285.

125 Foster 1999: 390.

126 Foster 2016: 404.

127 Foster 1999: 383.

128 Foster 1999: 381.

129 Foster 1999: 388.

130 Foster 1999; Marx K (1981) *Capital.* Vol. 3. London: Penguin, 949–950.

131 Marx 1976: 637–638.

132 Marx 1976: 323.

133 Moore JW (2011) Transcending the metabolic rift. *Journal of Peasant Studies* 38(1): 1–46 (2); Marx 1973: 748.

134 Moore 2011: 12.

135 Foster JB, Jermier JM, Shrivastava P (1997) Global environmental crisis and ecosocial reflection and inquiry. *Organization & Environment* 10(1): 5–11; Beacham J (2018) Organising food differently. *Organization* 25(4): 533–549;

Böhm S, Misoczky MC, Moog S (2012) Greening capitalism? *Organization Studies* 33(11): 1617–1638; Roux-Rosier A, Azambuja R, Islam G (2018) Alternative visions: Permaculture as imaginaries of the anthropocene. *Organization* 25(4): 550–572; Wright C, Nyberg D, Rickards L, Freund J (2018) Organizing in the anthropocene. *Organization* 25(4): 455–471.

136 Burkett 1996; Foster JB, Burkett P (2018) Value isn't everything. *Monthly Review* 70(1): 1–17.

137 Salleh A (2010) From metabolic rift to 'metabolic value'. *Organization & Environment* 23(2): 205–219.

138 Salleh 2010: 212.

139 Ergene S, Calás MB, Smircich L (2018) Ecologies of sustainable concerns. *Gender, Work & Organization* 25: 222–245.

140 Corvellec H, Böhm S, Stowell A, Valenzuela F (2020) Introduction to the special issue on the contested realities of the circular economy. *Culture and Organization* 26(2): 97–102; Valenzuela F, Böhm S (2017) Against wasted politics. *Ephemera: Theory & Politics in Organization* 17(1): 23–60; Genovese A, Pansera M (2020) The circular economy at a crossroads. *Capitalism Nature Socialism*. doi:10.1080/10455752.2020.1763414; Böhm S, Manolchev C, Pitts FH (2019) Circular economy from below: Labour, organising and the production of social and ecological innovation. Paper presented at the 37th International Labour Process Conference, University of Vienna, 24th April 2019; Bozkurt Ö, Stowell A (2016) Skills in the green economy. *New Technology, Work and Employment* 31(2): 146–160; Pettinger L (2017) Green collar work. *Sociology Compass*. doi:10.1111/soc4.12443; Laser S, Stowell A (2020) Thinking like Apple's recycling robots. *Ephemera* 20(2). Available at: www.ephemerajournal.org/contribution/thinking-apple%E2%80%99s-recycling-robots-toward-activation-responsibility-postenvironmentalist

141 Corvellec et al. 2020: 97–98, 100.

142 Valenzuela & Böhm 2017.

143 Valenzuela & Böhm 2017: 25–26, 42.

144 Corvallec et al. 2020: 98.

145 Laser & Stowell 2020.

146 Bozkurt & Stowell 2016; Pettinger 2017; Salleh 2010.

147 Valenzuela & Böhm 2017: 41.

148 Valenzuela & Böhm 2017: 44, 48.

149 Genovese & Pansera 2020.

150 Marx 1976: 915, stress added.

151 Cooke 2003; Banerjee 2008.

5 Conclusion

From the politics of value to the politics of work

Introduction

In concluding the book, we will consider the practical implications of the approaches to Marx's critique of political economy (CoPE) covered in preceding chapters for a new politics and public policy of value and work in the context of a changing capitalism. The process of completing this book was upended by successive crises, local and global, that made the sometimes obscure topic matter seem meagre and unimportant. The preceding chapters having cohered from piecemeal elements in the shadow of the pandemic, I am putting the finishing touches to this conclusion in the context of another cataclysmic crisis breaking upon the world stage: the Russian war against Ukraine. War, hot or cold, disrupts the capacity to enforce upon reality strict models of material determination. The struggles for recognition on which they rest, waged through and for supremacy or self-determination, defy the conceptual architecture of conventional rationalist explanations of social conflict, whether Marxist or mainstream.

Moreover, as economic and organisational life in the West and beyond becomes increasingly shaped by the imperative to combat Putin's expansionist programme of war crimes and imperialist aggression, there are significant limits on the capacity of the study of management and organisation alone to tell us anything meaningful about this rapidly unravelling world. First by means of the pandemic, and now by means of war and a new age of systemic competition between geopolitical rivals, economic life will be increasingly shaped by politics and the state, from the top down and probably not from the bottom up—at least not without a fight. Politics and the state are something we have touched upon repeatedly in this book, but they are phenomena that extant management and organisation studies (MOS), as well as extant Marxism, possess few useful or adaptable theoretical resources with which to analytically or practically register the shifts in their current role and character.

DOI: 10.4324/9781003198895-5

This has consequences for the institutional environment within which much MOS is incubated: management and business schools. A recent *Der Spiegel* interview with the historian Ivan Krastev, commenting on the implications of Russia's war on the Ukrainian people, was particularly thought-provoking in this regard. 'Because of the pandemic and this war, the state again plays a larger role', he argued. 'In the pandemic, it was the welfare state that cared for its citizens and kept them alive. In this war, it is the security state that doesn't just protect its citizens, but could also demand something from them: namely, the readiness to make sacrifices'. He goes on:

> A friend of mine works at one of the biggest business schools. I told him: Everything you are teaching is useless. Just as useless as teaching socialism studies was in 1990. The world of globalisation and free trade, in which the economy was only interested in bottom lines and not in politics, will be over.[1]

In this sense, the current crisis exposes a deeper-seated problem with the disciplinary and pedagogical apparatus constructed around the study of business, management and organisations: the lack of connection with politics and policy, which ultimately structure the terms on which the labour process and the valorisation process themselves proceed. Whilst it is not possible at this late stage to speak to the precise aspects in which this deficit is becoming apparent in the changing world around us, the book will conclude by offering some thoughts on the possible implications of the CoPE, and in particular its analysis of the articulation between labour and value, for how we connect politics with the traditional terrain of MOS—including, most importantly, the question of praxis or 'performativity'—which, as we saw in the Introduction, is a major concern of contemporary Critical Management Studies (CMS). In doing so, we will focus in particular on the issue of the future of work and workers, and its relationship with the broader view on value offered in this book.

Beyond productivism and distributionism

Together, the approaches covered in this book expose economic and managerial categories—for example, value—not simply as discursive, immaterial or abstract but as concretely grounded in an articulation of the social and the material, spanning relations of class, race, gender and the human metabolism with nature. In this way, rooting macro-economic categories of value, wealth and profit in a set of concrete, human relationships, this critical approach also exposes them as contingent. Against the naturalisation of a society organised around capital and the expansion of profit, the theories we encounter uncover the human social content and origins of apparently neutral and objective economic and technical categories. Laying bare this contingency and human content concealed in objective economic categories like value, the approaches encountered in this book perform the quintessential critical role of suggesting the possibility of alternative or improved ways of managing and organising work and economic life in response to the key challenges and crises facing society, humanity and the planet today. These approaches, and the understandings they generate of how value mediates life and labour in capitalist society, thus have much to say in answer to the question of praxis troubling MOS scholars today—both in their capacity to formulate a critique of capitalism and to envision practical means of socially de-mediating and re-mediating organisational and economic life in pursuit of alternatives. We live in a world where things are in question on the streets. At stake for the analyses examined here is the issue of how MOS scholars bring that questioning from the streets into the seminar room and reflect it more truthfully in the way that we understand the changing world of work and economic life.

Viewing value through labour, and labour through value, as two internally related parts of the production of wealth and value in capitalist society, enables a different perspective on some of the same problems addressed by the present-day politics of value propagated in the long period of populism following the fallout from the 2008 financial crisis, and imply different kinds of practical, organisational and policy response. By relating ideas of value to the workplace as the site where the things that carry value are produced and where claim is laid to the value of our labour, the theories charted in this book give us tools to understand how, rather than always reading work and economic life through the frame of the brand new thing, there are essential aspects that guarantee continuities in how we interpret, organise and contest the relationship between the labour process and the valorisation process in the contemporary time. The problem with work, on this count, is not that it is rendered subject to value. Rather there are fundamental aspects about work itself that need to be addressed by public policy, independent of the circulation, appropriation and distribution of the value it creates beyond the point of production.

Proposing a coming 'end of work' or 'post-work' society, popular ideas around the future of work have tended to underplay the wider political-economic context within which the workplace sits, and in particular how the latter is shaped by the forms and purposes associated with value.[2] In particular, much discussion of the future of work tends to focus on the potential of emerging technologies to reshape the workplace and employment relations. The technologies being available to reconfigure work, their implementation is taken to be a case of the specific character of the tasks that distinguish a given labour process, or its particular inputs and outputs. Whilst the central-ity of technology and work to current debates is understandable, somewhat less attention is paid to value itself as a specific social, political and eco-nomic category. This book has used the CoPE to understand the relationship between value and labour, or, more precisely, the valorisation process and the labour process. The labour process, through which the goods and services that carry value are produced, represents only one part of the valorisation process as the overall set of relationships through which a return is earned on invested capital, a surplus generated, and wealth accumulated from the production of commodified goods and services. Considerations of the rela-tive cost and benefit of investing in new shopfloor technologies based on market conditions and competitive pressures, for instance, play a crucial role in shaping or constraining how the future of work unfolds.

In a developed and complex capitalist economy, the labour process is not a simple one, geared solely towards the satisfaction of human needs and wants. Rather it is one organised by the pursuit of profit—in other words, the valorisation of value through the production of commodities exchanged on markets for money. Meanwhile, value, expressed in the price of labour via the wage, is also a medium for the recognition of our work in such a soci-ety. In both these respects, it is important to understand the future of work through the prism of value. In this book, value has been understood as the relationship between things, and between people and things, expressed in money and prices. Through the exchange of goods and services for money, it articulates what goes on in the workplace with what goes on in the market—and vice versa, structuring the character and experience of labour. What the theories traversed in this book suggest is that an application of Marx's CoPE too focused on the 'hidden abode' of production results in an overly 'pro-ductivist' approach to the future of work focused narrowly on the problem of work at the expense of an engagement with broader set of relations that constitute value.

'Productivism' is often expressed politically in what Moishe Postone describes as 'a normative critique of non-productive social groupings from the standpoint of those groupings that are "truly" productive'.[3] As we saw in the introduction, this normative critique reappeared in the populist move-ments of left and right that emerged following the 2008 financial crisis, which took productiveness as a 'criterion of social worth' in critiquing 'greedy bankers' and international financial institutions. In the age of 'aus-terity populism'—where centre-right governments scrutinised so-called 'benefit scroungers' and welfare claimants as symbolic of unproduc-tive activity and expenditure perceived as having caused the crisis—this productivist politics of value helped shape a radical discourse around the relationship between the labour process and the valorisation process.[4] Significant cuts having been made to the welfare budget, and the argument for austerity having been effectively won at the ballot box, subsequently this search for unproductive forces who could be held responsible for the ills of contemporary capitalism passed over into national populism. This was characterised by the identification of apparent external forces like migrants and international institutions as exerting a leeching, parasitical drain on the productiveness of the national community of hard-working people. This sometimes played out in a theorisation of value as an objective category belonging to particular people and places competed over in a zero-sum game waged between increasingly protectionist and nationalist economies.

Elements of this imaginary were also picked up by the left over this period, specifically where value was understood as properly resting within localities, the aim of public policy being to preserve and protect its realisation by the communities themselves rather than it leaking away into the monetary system at large—expressed in initiatives such as local currencies. These alternatives exhibit some of the same weaknesses open Marxists have noted of attempts to create new communities around money, as discussed in the first section of Chapter 4. On the left in particular, this way of understanding value post-crisis also intersected with a critique of the monetary abstraction forced upon the 'real' economy by global finance. Whilst the response of the right to a similar assessment has been to seek various means of 'deglobalising' economies towards more nationally oriented production and supply chains, for a left largely out of power this reading has often resulted in a critique of financialisation and globalisation that can lapse into conspiracy theories about greedy, corrupt bankers and other elites who infringe upon the value-productiveness of a pristine 'people'.

Whilst the widespread defeat of left populism and the waning of financialised neoliberalism suggest the political neutralisation of this critique, it has arguably passed over into a new and much more specific and sophisticated form in contemporary radical thinking about the uneven influence of rents and rentier dynamics in the modern economy, as we saw in Chapter 3. In particular, this focuses on the divergent impacts of an asset-driven mode of accumulation on different age groups—the 'production boundary' shifting once again to place new groups on the wrong side of the line separating productiveness from unproductiveness. In common with critiques of financialised capitalism following the 2008 crisis, today's critiques of rentier elites also centre on how capital seeks opportunities to accumulate through apparently unproductive routes that ultimately act as a drag on investment in the productive 'real' economy.

Overly focused on identifying the location of the 'hidden abode' and remunerating those who reside there, productivist understandings of value find a dialectical mirror image where they pass over into 'distribution-ist' approaches to organising and regulating economic life—applications of which are at once far too focused on economic life *beyond* the hidden abode, engaging with the problem of value whilst eliding the centrality of work in capitalist society. At a policy and organisational level, distribution-ism focuses on the provision of cash transfers to address or mitigate what it perceives as the ill effects of capitalist economics. As Martin Hagglund argues, the contemporary 'emancipatory vision', left, right and centre, seems 'restricted to the redistribution of wealth, while blind to the fundamental question of how wealth is produced under capitalism'. From 'the social democratic welfare state' to 'advocates for a universal basic income', there remains a fixation on the 'mode of distribution' of capitalist wealth alone.[5]

Rather than anything specific to the work that produces the goods and services that carry value and generate a profit, distributionist accounts see the issue with our economy as being the means through which the value and profit is expressed and the way it is distributed. In this way, what we might call 'productivism' and 'distributionism' represent two sides of the same coin insofar as a focus on work and a focus on value taken in isolation tend to naturalise and seal off from scrutiny the other. The unintended con-sequences of these political understandings of value is that, critiquing the sphere of circulation alone, they actually end up rhetorically and analyti-cally preserving the labour process as an unchanging principle to which other economic phenomena stand in a purely external relation.

For Robert Kurz, critiques of capitalist social relations that focus only on how those relations are mediated in the social forms specific to circula-tion imply a traditional Marxist 'labour ontology' reliant on a transhistorical understanding of labour as a pure and untouched concrete principle around which abstractions circulate in the market alone. The problem for such critiques, in this sense, is not really labour, but the forms of exchange, distribution and ownership that surround it. In this sense, the relations of production are theoretically folded into property relations alone, reduced to the juridical relationship between the buyer and seller of labour power. Thus the status of production itself as a real and practical abstraction is left untouched. Because the exchange abstraction—the alleged problem with capitalism—is seen as consisting only in circulation, this means that 'circu-lationist' strands of Marxian value theory are no better than the productivist approaches of traditional Marxism and their suspicion of 'unproductive' forces like finance infringing upon the 'real' economy. The external rela-tion this presupposes between concrete production and abstract circulation mimics the traditional critique of capitalism offered by 'labour movement Marxism', insofar as production is left untroubled by critique and the problem of capitalism is instead seen to pertain to circulation alone. The circulationist preoccupation with the sphere of exchange leaving the sphere of production pristinely intact, the only explanatory framework left to them through which to understand production in capitalist society is little more than a radical spin on Weber's 'Protestant ethic'. Such an approach falsely ontologises labour as concrete, insofar as it is associated with an unchanging physiological expenditure logically and historically prior to its abstraction according to the specific historical guise its mediation assumes at different points in time—i.e. by monetary exchange in capitalist society. But capitalist valorisation, Kurz writes, is not an 'unkosher' imposition on the production of useful things as the naturalistic worldview of traditional Marxism and its sometimes unwitting descendants might suggest. Abstract labour, for Kurz, is not a non-substantial 'validation relation' forged in circulation, but a relation of production and a substantial relation of subjugation', and as such centres on the production process as itself a 'real abstraction' not only bearing a material and physical content, but social content too. Hence it at once produces a spectral and 'ghostlike' objectivity—value—whilst also implying intense and deleterious consequences for resources both human and natural. Approaches that seek to banish this spectral, ghostlike character solely to the circulation process alone miss the historical and social specificity of capitalism and naturalise production as a real abstraction, mistaking it for concrete labour pure and simple.[6]

As such, it is important to see labour and value as internally connected rather than externally imposed upon one another, the latter perspective obscuring the very real interconnection between the workplace and production on one hand and the circulation and distribution of value on the other. For instance, rather than financialisation and rentierisation being seen as sapping the life from the 'real' economy, sparking a productivity crisis, shifting the critique from the valorisation process to the labour process flips this understanding insofar as financialisation and rentierisation appear as responses to underlying difficulties in the production of wealth and value itself. The greater manufacturing capacity created by the opening up of the world economy into the 1970s saw overproduction blight profitability and send capital seeking returns through other routes such as through speculative channels of investment and revenue-raising.[7] The rise of a share-holder-driven model of financialised capitalism did of course exacerbate the underpinning productivity crisis by incentivising the payment of dividends from profits that otherwise might have been reinvested in upgrading, but, as the approaches covered in Chapter 2 tell us, financialisation and, later, rentierisation were an outgrowth of problems at the point of production rather than representing an alien imposition that themselves caused problems in production in turn. The critique of the sphere of circulation and distribution alone leaves untouched how the real consequences of financialisation and rentierisation have been felt and experienced at the point of production—as demonstrated by Labour Process Theory's recent engagements with how 'value logics' play out on the shopfloor, examined earlier in this book.

Putting politics back into the critique of political economy

These arguments are not an abstract theoretical exercise but have implications for policy and both organisational and political praxis. Theories of value, whilst often abstract, have played a major part in 'defining the politics of the last few centuries'.[8] This has tended to inform a politics based on the distribution of the fruits of production rather than a more fundamental reconfiguration of the architecture of work and economic life through a focus on labour relations. Such distributionist perspectives have their roots in the classical political economy of Smith and Ricardo, who focused the study of the economy on production, over which was layered an understanding of the distribution and exchange relations through which the surplus generated is appropriated and distributed between classes. The political implications of their understanding of value as physically embodied in commodities by labour were to recommend the redistribution of that value as a mode of class reconciliation. The surplus having been created by labour, it then becomes a case of workers laying claim to a greater slice of the pie following its production, rather than having a stake in the pie itself. Policy-wise, this has rested on the assumption that capitalism would generate the levels of growth capable of facilitating redistribution of the proceeds. Through the technocratic generation of social democrats that led Western governments in the middle part of the twentieth century, this became a core part of the 'labourist' policy arsenal, steered by a large, bureaucratic state.

This economistic approach continued as, later in the century and into the next, governments and labour movements were confronted by an economy experiencing the consequences of deindustrialisation and global competition, including a decline in real wages and disposable income. Rather than employment regulation and an extension of collective bargaining, tweaks to the tax system were seen as sufficient to support workers in a service-based economy. Globalisation and financialisation were expected to deliver economic dividends that could then be redistributed to workers as benefits and tax credits to compensate them for wider effects on the economy and buttress low wages. This promised workers ameliorative cash transfers from the state rather than attempting to improve working life at the coalface by granting workers the power and capacity to lay claim to value in and prior to production. These 'remedial cash transfers' left untouched 'fundamental design questions in the nature of modern capitalism' and unchallenged its 'associated degradations'. The focus remained on 'how you chop up the proceeds of growth rather than redesigning the system itself'.[9]

This was partly a result of the 2008 financial crisis giving rise to a more critical strand of distributionism imported into the corridors of power from the radical movements that filled the streets and squares in the wake of the crash. One of the most famous and influential treatments of the distribution of value as the specific problem with contemporary capitalism was that of Thomas Piketty. Articulating a critique of the so-called '99%' against which the Occupy movement railed, Piketty's work represented what Hagglund calls 'a paradigmatic example of a social democratic critique of neoliberal capitalism', in that the policy programme that flowed from its diagnosis of capitalism's ills 'centred on redistribution' rather than the character and organisation of work itself.[10] The likes of Piketty tend to focus on the disproportionate rate of return from wealth compared to underlying economic growth. The focus has tended therefore to fall on the relationships of distribution through which the so-called 1% accrue a larger slice of the pie as the explanation for capitalism's malaise. The underpinning productive dynamics that hamstring economic growth are given much less attention as a site for the redress of these issues and a wider balancing of the economy.

The idea that the 'real economy' of productive labour was infringed by financial abstraction, and that the solution to the age of austerity was a greater level of state intervention or ownership within the context of essentially the same set of production relations, informed the left's politics of value in the wake of the 2008 crisis. The translation of elements of Occupy and other 'anti-austerity' political movements into left-populist electoral projects saw this distributionist perspective continue to structure left policy-making. The increasing attraction of a 'fully automated' vision of the future where, with an impending 'end of work', work and workers were no longer relevant, served to disincentivise serious thought about policy interventions into the employment relation itself, and led to calls for cash transfers on an even wider scale to hold economic life together as a society based on wage labour waned. Going beyond the familiar toolkit of tax credits, the ameliorative measures proposed by those anticipating or willing an imminent 'end of work' assumed the utopian guise of the universal basic income.

A preoccupation with these fashionable distributional alternatives left untouched the foundations of the increasingly insecure labour market and unrewarding workplace that emerged in the long post-crisis period. With the wage-labour relationship weakened by unemployment and the crash exacerbating low growth, this era of austerity populism had appeared to sharpen distributional conflicts, including along generational lines. The new context of national-populist revolt these conditions helped incubate saw centre-left policymakers respond by once again returning to proposal of policies focused on the provision of cash transfers to address or mitigate the perceived ill effects of capitalist economics. As policymakers attempted to work with a smaller overall economic pie, left and right alike threw themselves into placing 'political primacy' on 'distributional battles' between warring parties rather than a common attempt to address the 'character of work itself'.[11] With an emptied-out system of industrial relations depriving the economy of any countervailing power capable of commanding gains from below, policymakers on left and right alike were left with little choice but to attempt to 'co-opt alienated populist voters' with impossible and ineffective 'after-tax redistribution schemes'. Purporting to iron out contradictions produced by the neoliberal era, rather than fundamentally confronting the underlying relations of work and production, these would simply seek to 'reconcile voters to an unchanged economic order'.[12]

As Postone argues, distributionism's selective approach has 'serious weaknesses and consequences', isolating the valorisation process as an object of policymaking from its relationship with the labour process and vice versa.[13] Adopting the standpoint of a pristine sphere of production to make a moral claim about the negative influence exerted upon it by the apparently corruptive class character of capitalist society, much left critique of contemporary capitalism has tended to view the pursuit of profit as a kind of conspiracy of 'corporate elites' seeking to appropriate the wealth produced by society, rather than a structural imperative to which we are all subject. The labour process through which the 'real economy' of goods and services is generated is not a victim of unnecessary abstract compulsions forced upon it by the pursuit of profit and the valorisation of value. Growth is the *purpose* of our economy, on which our work and lives depend, and not some 'ideology' from which we can freely rid ourselves. As Hagglund writes, 'the defining purpose of capital accumulation is built into how we produce our social wealth in the first place', rather than being an imposition upon it.[14] This interconnection is placed out of view by accounts narrowly focused on labour or value alone—perhaps because it renders more difficult the proposal of various panaceas by policymakers, requiring a more complex set of compromises between labour, capital and the state.

By rhetorically and politically preserving labour and production, the policies that flow from distributionist critiques also operate on fundamentally mistaken assumptions about the capacity of the economy to sustain the amelioration of capitalism's ills that they promise voters and workers. Hagglund gives the example of how the basic income claims to obviate workers of the need to work, but simultaneously remains as dependent as any other form of cash transfer on the redistribution of wealth generated by the same set of productive relations. As such, the measure undermines the bold claims of a fundamental break with work attached to it by some of its more radical proponents precisely by depending upon the thing whose necessity it purports to negate. The contradiction, here, is that the less we live our lives in line with the exploitation of our labour power, the less of a fiscal basis there is for the kind of redistributive welfare state the universal basic income would represent.

Moreover, the funding of these transfers via the tax take depends upon a productive dynamism entirely lacking in many contemporary economies. In most modern redistributive schemes, this has been made up for through reliance on financial services and asset bubbles, making for an unstable foundation on which to base durable redistributive policies. In recent times, speculative and service-driven Western economies have rested on offshoring and exploiting low-cost labour and satisfying shareholder value—neither of which provides a conducive basis for stimulating investment in techniques and technologies to aid the domestic productivity revival that could underpin such redistributive mechanisms. Where asset and financial bubbles made such a bargain possible for social democratic governments offering in-work and out-of-work benefits to voters in the 1990s and early noughties, the crisis of neoliberalism and the persistent lack of underlying productive dynamism in the contemporary economy calls the capacity to fund these schemes into question. Funded on the basis of these unstable foundations, measures like tax credits have typically stood in for policies aimed at regulating and dignifying labour. They subsidised the capacity of employers to operate low-wage, low-productivity workplaces where intensification substituted for innovation, exacerbating factors associated with the populist grievances that delivered Trump, Brexit and the rest. Failing to address the conditions under which wealth and value are produced, and dealing only with their distribution after the fact, cash transfer schemes sought to 'respond to working-class populist rebellions by offering workers the chance to become something other than workers', leaving unexplored avenues through which workers could address insecurity and anxiety by bargaining through their work for better.[15]

In spite of this interconnection between narrowly distributive policies and the growth of the populist politics of grievance, a distributionist perspective has nonetheless continued to structure how policymakers have sought to respond to the political issue of winning back the support of working-class voters in so-called 'left behind' post-industrial communities. Viewing material factors alone as the secret of their grievances, policy programmes have proposed to remedy the woes of working-class communities through 'distributive justice'. Whilst welcome, distributional measures are ultimately indifferent to the roots of the anger and resentment that underpins populist discontent in 'the wider emotional wellbeing of citizens' and their hopes and aspirations for the 'lives they wish to live'.[16] In this sense, it is insufficient to simply remunerate those deemed to have lost out to globalisation through 'concessions to national working-class economic interests' alone, without also addressing cultural, emotional and political issues around power and control.[17] The 'economistic' character of distributionist approaches focuses on action at the level of the state rather than 'questions of power and democracy' at the level of the workplace and community.[18] Against the proposal of redistribution as a panacea for the economic drivers of populist discontent, there is a longstanding tendency among 'labour liberals and social democrats', when given a choice, to oppose 'post-tax transfers of cash to individuals'. In the face of unfavourable economic conditions and unconvincing policy propositions, then, what is needed instead is a politics of work and value that can address the articulation of the labour process and the valorisation process together.[19] The theories covered in this book provide different, and in some ways complementary, perspectives towards this end, but the tools provided by Marx and Marxists alone can only take us so far. Indeed, we will close by considering how the search for alternatives may actually necessitate the reconnection of the CoPE with some of the discursive and ethical terrain addressed by CMS and other less materialist and economistic strands of the study of work and organisation in recent decades.

Struggles for recognition and the revaluation of value

The new directions in the application of Marx's CoPE in MOS presented here offer a theoretical approach that can help conceptually reconnect subjective processes of identification, which have traditionally been at the core of CMS, to the social relations structuring work and society under capitalism. This body of theory allows the examination of specific forms of subjectivity and identity as part and parcel of the struggle surrounding the social mediation of labour both in the workplace and in market exchange, rather than as solely located outside it on some separate plane of the symbolic constitution of the self. By emphasising the foundational role of dispossession and coercion in the maintenance of class relations, and the role of market exchange in validating different kinds of labour power and concrete labour as valuable and socially necessary, these new directions recover attention for the structural, material and collective dimensions of control and resistance under capitalism, restoring balance to the study of conflict and antagonism in CMS.

CMS has accurately captured how the rhetorical and ideological construction and valuation of different identities and subjectivities act as an important modality through which control operates in capitalist society. But the applications of Marx's CoPE covered in Chapters 2–4 enable us to see that socio-ideological control rarely occurs without more 'direct' forms of control such as bureaucratic rules, surveillance and technological intensification, and is necessarily predicated on commodified labour. Such dimensions cannot thus be simply evaded or relegated to the 'context' within which socio-ideological control occurs, but should rather be fully theorised as co-constitutive of it. Workers may be highly dependent on commodified work for their own sense of self and social meaning, but what the approaches presented here underwrite is that, under capitalism, they are also dependent on it for their subsistence. Ignoring this mystifies the classed structure of society leading to a critical scholarship centred on what has been tellingly called 'decaf resistance', or a resistance that 'threatens and hurts nobody . . . resistance without a cost', stuck within the individualised self produced through capitalist governmentality.[20]

At the same time, it is nonetheless necessary to reconnect the CoPE with the political and non-material aspects of human work and the processes through which worth is placed on people, activities and things. CMS may provide a suitable context within which to start doing some of this on an academic and theoretical basis, but the analyses of value offered in the preceding chapters also speak to some of the pressing practical and political issues of creating paths of resistance and opening up the possibility of alternatives in and out of contemporary society. In this sense, whilst wages are an important part of the struggle for the recognition of the value of one's labour, and, as Chapter 4 of this book has demonstrated, conflicts over identity and difference are themselves intertwined with the articulation of the material with the social represented in value as a form of mediation, it is also essential that any politics of value accommodates the struggle for the non-material forms of recognition that characterise the human relationship with work across those lines of identity and difference. Value is not solely objective, nor solely subjective, but abstracts from and mediates a conflicted relationship between the two. We can turn to Marx to understand that value is an objectification of subjective activity and desire, an abstract form assumed by concrete human practice in which the latter is often hidden or unrecognisable to us. Take, for instance, how important forms of work such as health and care services are often poorly remunerated, how the remuneration of those forms of work is imbricated with the positionalities of those performing it, or how the way our work is measured conflicts with how we experience it. Marx, and Marxian theory, still represents the lodestar for understanding a world where value shapes the management and organisation of work. It is a key insight of many of the Marxian approaches brought together here that, as a form in which our subjective activity is objectified, value expresses not anything intrinsic to people, places and things, but rather the abstract relationship between them, represented in money, and that has implications for the practice and experience of work.

In this way, 'abstract' labour represented in value is not something imposed upon workers, and 'concrete' labour unburdened by value does not represent a principle of resistance to it.[21] Such a view would ontologically essentialise class struggle in such a way as to pose it as independent of or prior to the value-form, rather than recognising that workers themselves personify the pursuit of surplus-value as bearers of the commodity labour power, and social conflicts emerge from this context rather than having an existence strictly independent of it. The needs of workers are not a pole of opposition to capital, so much as the expression of a productive subjectivity historically specific to it. Moreover, power in capitalist society is often indirect and impersonal, centred on a process of social mediation to which all humans in capitalist society are subject, whether owners of capital or owners of labour power.[22] Neglecting the need for struggles to work in and through these forms of social mediation in turn leads to a 'spontaneist' understanding of resistance harboured in the search for a dignified form of concrete labour that can be isolated as a counterpoint to the value abstraction. The task instead, for those wanting to dignify labour through a struggle over the terms of value, is to work through both abstract and concrete, objective and subjective, economic and political at once.

By seeing 'abstract' market forces as an unacceptable imposition upon the 'concrete' sphere of production, approaches that focus alone on relations of distribution and circulation as the problem with capitalism get us no closer to these aspects of social mediation and class struggle in a society organised around value. Confronted by purely subjective theories of value and the objective theories of value that, as we saw in the Introduction, are implicitly espoused by populists and others, the truth, as always, lies somewhere in between, and it is necessary to walk the line between both poles. Among current policy and organisational responses, something like a politics of *recognition* may have the capacity to straddle this distinction, providing a basis for the practical occupation of the terrain of power, control and identity on which contemporary political conflicts have played out, rather than seeking to artificially cleanse the world of these conflicts by means of state payments and impotent assaults on market forces.

The language of labour and value sometimes leaves little space to engage with the emotional aspects of work and economic life that have driven the age of populism. Economically determinist worldviews like that of classical political economy and traditional Marxism have few conceptual resources to capture how social and economic phenomena are driven by non-material factors, and in particular the struggle for the recognition of our dignity at work and elsewhere. As Francis Fukuyama argues his much-maligned and much-misunderstood book *The End of History and the Last Man*, rather than calculating reason or material desire, humankind is distinguished by moral choice, and in particular the capacity to value and esteem things. This moral dimension compels humans to pursue recognition, and means that social and political phenomena cannot simply be reduced to 'the mechanics of matter in motion', nor 'a competition for power between economic interests'. Rather than configuring our political economy to ensure 'mutual non-aggression' between vying economic interests in the name of 'material comfort' alone, our political economy must create routes for the 'recognition of dignity and worth' by different actors.[23] In liberal societies, this recognition can be facilitated through 'mediating institutions' that sit between the individual and the state, including trade unions.[24] To illustrate how recognition is mediated in contemporary society, Fukuyama uses the example of an industrial dispute. Material desire is not the sole driver of why workers enter into dispute with employers. Rather, the struggle for higher wages or better terms and conditions is also a struggle for the recognition of the worth, value and dignity of the workers and their work. These struggles cannot be explained solely through reference to the 'complex set of desires that make up physical existence', but rather use bargaining over material gains to further the satisfaction of a form of recognition that exceeds economic concerns alone and centres instead on the pursuit of dignity.[25]

This alternative understanding of value therefore opens up the possibility of other means of making a better future of work reality. In particular, the concept of recognition helps bring into focus the character of value as an open and contingent category of struggle combining social and economic, subjective and objective aspects. But, as Fukuyama argues, the development of liberal society always runs the risk of squeezing out the key human capacity to esteem things and activities on the basis of their worth and dignity, increasingly tending to structure policymaking and economic decision-making around a narrowly rationalist and calculating approach to value as an economic category alone. The economic obstruction of channels for social and political processes of recognition and valuation means that the struggle for recognition can take ever more vexed and unpredictable forms—as witnessed in the populist politics of grievance that has characterised the last decade. This means that new institutional mediations and forms of association are necessary to reconnect the politics of work and the politics of value.

Of course, Kurz is right to note the limited character of a politics of work bound to the 'struggle for recognition' on the terrain of value alone. As he notes, such a politics necessarily represents an acceptance of the constraints of a kind of 'iron cage' imposing the economic rationality upon struggles waged for an improved position within what remains essentially the same system of social relations. Laying claims to value, workers seek recognition as 'subjects, legal persons and citizens' imprisoned within the 'fetish form', with politics 'the vehicle for this restriction'. But where Kurz casts this modus operandi of the labour movement in a wholly negative light, it also provides a durable template for how workers can find room to move within the value-form, in the absence of any other alternative.[26]

One way in which this could be achieved is through a reenvisioning of the role of trade unions in the economy. Workers have historically tended to express a preference for measures that increase their ability of workers to 'bargain for higher pre-tax wages' rather than draw down cash transfers from the state. Granting workers 'genuine economic bargaining power', as well as new forms of 'countervailing power' in the political sphere, would intervene in how the cake is baked and not simply how it is cut and sliced. At present, where collective bargaining is in evidence in liberal market economies, it is in the form of 'enterprise bargaining' organised at a plant-by-plant level. This limits the generalisability of agreements across sectors and makes for a poor match between the tradition repertoires of dispute resolution available to workers and the particular conditions of the service-based work that dominates Western economies. Frameworks like sectoral wage boards or Fair Pay Agreements, meanwhile, project a different and potentially more effective way forward—and would also, in an age of inflationary pressures, enable workers to command payrises more in line with sharp increases in the cost of living. Going further, a 'restoration of tripartite bargaining' between labour, capital and the state could further enable workers to contest the terms on which their work and the world are valued, rather than treating the labour process as a static and unchanging element around which policy must be organised.[27]

Were favourable political and economic conditions in place—perhaps, as previously, owing to new systemic competition on a global scale—this could resemble the 'counterpower' that Hardt and Negri see represented in the 'free worker institutions' that regulated the capital–labour antagonism in the Fordist-Keynesian class compromise. As witnessed in Chapter 3, the workerist tradition has long fixated on the limited but nonetheless meaningful gains achieved by the mass worker in the context of the New Deal and other reformist compacts. Hardt and Negri recommend that today too 'democratic institutions must organize counterpowers and keen open and plural the developments of constituent power' along the lines of that afforded in the stimulation of labour organisation and collective bargaining that anchored twentieth-century capitalist economies. This they present as a means for capitalism to be reformed from below, and a path to possibly circumvent the historical association they note between traditional socialism and the simple seizing of an unreconstructed state power in the name of the 'public' in order to steer an ultimately unchanged productive apparatus. The statist turn on the contemporary post-crisis left, whilst 'eminently pragmatic' in their view, seeks an 'unrealistic' alternative to 'neoliberal globalization' in the absence of the objective material conditions that made Keynesianism and state socialism possible in the twentieth century. Instead, they call for 'non-state public power' comprising 'non-sovereign' institutions that can retain the dynamic movement between power and plural counterpowers, and do not posit their eventual resolution in a sovereign power to rule over 'society and the state'—although, of course, this may entail seizing power concentrated in the state in order to give it away in the first place. Rather than withdrawing into the nation, this would also hold open the possibility of contesting the rule of value at the level of the 'capitalist world market' and its intractably global character.[28]

By opening up channels for the recognition of value socially and economically, the revitalisation of 'free worker institutions' such as unions sitting independent of both capital and the state would also create the possibility of the 'revaluation of value' that Hagglund proposes.[29] Whereas across the social democratic political spectrum redistribution has been seen as a solution to the distribution of wealth, what is required is 'a challenge to the measure of value that shapes our production of wealth' itself, and thus 'the form in which our economic relations appear'. Through the extension of collective bargaining, strengthening of worker voice, and granting workers space to organise according to the specificity of their jobs and industries, the values and measures to which work is subject can be cracked open and reconfigured. This would remove the veil on value as an economic category and reveal it as a social, political and institutional principle combining both objective and subjective elements.

The revaluation Hagglund proposes seeks to stimulate new objectifications of our subjective activity that, whilst inevitably abstract and alienated from our practical experience of the world, may mark an improvement on the forms through which our relations are mediated today. The pandemic and the ensuing health, social and economic crisis it sparked have already begun a revaluation of the value of forms of work that were previously underpaid and neglected, now newly revealed as central to society's subsistence and reproduction. The struggle now is for our forms of value to accurately capture the new status of those workers classed as 'essential' in the crisis, spanning everything from retail to waste and elderly care to education. This is a political question, rather than purely economic one, and will require organisation and regulation. But whilst this might represent a shift in the politics of value, value's compulsive power to determine how and what we prioritise in life will remain undiminished. Even as it misrepresents the world to us, ordering our lives against our wills, we depend upon value's expansion and growth to live, work and subsist. This compels us to act against ourselves and others in support of a system constructed on our own exploitation, for justified fear of failure, economic collapse and the far worse alternatives that may lie in wait beyond it. Something along the lines of Hagglund's 'revaluation of value' would create room to contest, create and institutionalise other ways of valuing what we prioritise and place worth on in the context of the mutual human finitude we share and which was so cruelly exposed as the pandemic tore through society.

***

For the time being at least, and in the absence of any plausible or desirable alternative to a world that must currently be defended against something far worse, it is sadly in all our interests to continue expanding and valorising economic value for the sake of our societies and selves. But, in the context of a long epoch of continuous, multisided and manifold crises, the status quo constitutes just the basis for the long process of rebuilding the subjective relationships that value expresses, remaking the notions of value that determine what we prioritise, and rethinking the objective forms in which that value appears. Rather than a reversion to the concrete and objective aspects of value against the abstract and subjective, the struggle is to reconnect them so that the one more accurately reflects the other. In this sense, a politics of value without a politics of work is worthless—and vice versa. It is therefore important that the prevailing politics of value is augmented with a new politics of work. This would articulate between the labour process and the valorisation process by means of new institutional mediations that provide a context for both recognition and revaluation. In short, we need to focus on the conditions under which wealth and value are produced—and not only on how they are distributed.

Notes

1 Krastev I (2022) Putin lives in historic analogies and metaphors. *Der Spiegel*, 17 March. Available at: www.spiegel.de/international/world/ivan-krastev-on-russia-s-invasion-of-ukraine-putin-lives-in-historic-analogies-and-metaphors-a-1d043090-1111-4829-be90-c20fd5786288

2 Dinerstein A, Pitts FH (2020) *A World Beyond Work?* Bingley: Emerald.

3 Postone M (1993) *Time, Labor, and Social Domination*. Cambridge: Cambridge University Press, 64–65.

4 Bolton M, Pitts FH (2018) *Corbynism: A Critical Approach*. Bingley: Emerald.

5 Hagglund M (2020) *This Life*. New York: Anchor, 287.

6 Kurz R (2016) *The Substance of Capital*. London: Chronos, 112, 196–99, 206.

7 Brenner R (2006) *The Economics of Global Turbulence*. London: Verso.

8 Cruddas J (2021) *The Dignity of Labour*. Cambridge: Polity.

9 Cruddas J, Pitts FH (2021) The labour party and the future of work. *Renewal*, 8–12 June. Available at: https://renewal.org.uk/labour-and-the-future-of-work-1/

10 Hagglund 2020: 288.
11 Cruddas & Pitts 2021.
12 Lind M (2020) *New Class War*. New York: Atlantic.
13 Postone 1993: 66.
14 Hagglund 2020.
15 Lind 2020: 122–124.
16 Cruddas 2021: 158–159, 188.
17 Lind 2020: 122–124.
18 Cruddas 2021: 134.
19 Lind 2020: 122–124.
20 Contu A (2008) Decaf resistance. *Management Communication Quarterly* 21: 364–379 (370).
21 Kicillof A, Starosta G (2007) Value form and class struggle. *Capital & Class* 31(2): 13–40.
22 Kicillof & Starosta 2007: 28.
23 Fukuyama F (2012) *The End of History and the Last Man*. London: Penguin, 151–152.
24 Fukuyama 2012: 322.
25 Fukuyama 2012: 172–173.
26 Kurz 2016: 174–5.
27 Lind 2021: 127–129.
28 Hardt M, Negri A (2017) *Assembly*. Oxford: Oxford University Press, 26, 32–43, 256–263.
29 Hagglund 2020: 262–267.

Index

140   *Index*

Printed in the United States
by Baker & Taylor Publisher Services